The Enquiring Classroom

3

15

The Enquiring Classroom:

AN APPROACH TO UNDERSTANDING CHILDREN'S LEARNING

Stephen Rowland

 The Falmer Press

A member of the Taylor & Francis Group
London and New York

UK The Falmer Press, Falmer House, Barcombe, Lewes, East Sussex, BN8 5DL

USA The Falmer Press, Taylor & Francis Inc., 242 Cherry Street, Philadelphia, PA 19106-1906

First published 1984. Reprinted 1987, 1988, 1990

Library of Congress Cataloging in Publication Data

Rowland, Stephen.
  The enquiring classroom.

  Includes bibliographical references.
  1. Merton Primary School. 2. Open plan schools—England—Syston (Leicestershire). 3. Teacher-student relationships—England—Syston (Leicestershire).
  I. Title.
  LF795.S975R69 1984 372.11′02 84-1480
  ISBN 0-905273-99-0 (pbk.)

Phototypeset in 11/12 Caledonia by
Imago Publishing Ltd, Thame, Oxon

Printed in Great Britain by Taylor & Francis (Printers) Ltd, Basingstoke

Contents

Acknowledgements

For adults, as for children, learning is a struggle to be enjoyed. Those who teach us most are those who open our eyes to the enjoyment of that struggle. I wish to thank those who have helped me to that enjoyment: Mary Brown, the headteacher of Sherard Primary School, where I taught for four years and learned to care for children; Michael Armstrong, whose insight opened up ways of understanding them; and Ann Taber, Jeni Smith, John Crookes, Peter Gilbert, Mary Ockwell, Alain Welch and Jim Nind, among others who shared their own investigations with me and so helped me to sharpen my ideas.

Then there were those without whom this enquiry would not have been possible: Chris Harris, who contributed to my understanding of the children from day to day, and whose classroom provided an open and thoughtful setting for the project; Stuart Ball, the headteacher at Merton School, who gave unfailing support for what I was doing in his school; Brian Cruickshank and Andrew Fairbairn who gave me every encouragement from Leicestershire Education Department; and Brian Simon, of Leicester University, whose sympathetic understanding and interest gave me the confidence to seek a wider audience with whom to share our work.

This book makes wide use of the work of the children in Chris Harris's class. I am indebted to them for this, and would especially like to thank those children and their parents who, some four years after I worked with them, discussed with me my plans for this book and the part their individual stories, inventions and discussions would play in it.

Finally, my gratitude to Gillian Rowland is incalculable. She has carefully read all the drafts for this book, has constructively criticized them at every level from the choice of a word to the formation of an argument, and has helped me to tread that narrow line between enthusiasm and obsession.

Chapter 1

Introduction: A Framework For Classroom Enquiry

This book offers an insight into the work of a group of children in a primary school classroom and is about how we, as classroom teachers must share and carefully analyze our experience of children if we are to develop our expertise with understanding, rather than passively respond to the 'educational' fads of the day. It is also an attempt to bring together the richness of the anecdote of classroom life and the intellectual scrutiny of the research project.

A theme that will recur in different forms throughout this book is the idea that at the heart of any good teaching and learning experience is a critical relationship, that is, a relationship in which teachers and learners alike seek to question each other's ideas, to reinterpret them, to adapt them and even to reject them, but not to discount them. To be critical in this sense, we need to know something of the origins of those ideas, their roots, the frameworks in which they are embedded. Furthermore, if this book is itself to be part of such a critical process, I must provide some outline of the origins of the ideas upon which it is based. To put this another way, the pictures of classroom life that I shall portray need to be given a frame, if others are to make use of them.

In order to provide this frame, it is necessary not only to outline the school context in which the events and observations took place, but also to say a word about myself as observer, my concerns, values and ideas. It is quite obvious that any two observers — and especially any two teachers — presented with the same classroom event, will perceive different things. For example, a piece of writing that strikes one teacher as showing a poor grasp of grammatical conventions, for another may be evidence of ingenuity in self-expression.

This essentially subjective way in which we interpret the classroom and children's activities within it has been considered by many educational researchers to be something to be avoided at all costs.[1] The 'unreliable' accounts of teachers have been dismissed in favour of such technical devices as observation schedules listing categories of behaviour to be noted and ticked off at regular intervals,[2] and questionnaires and tests whose results can be subjected to statistical analysis. But the claim to objectivity for any such devices must always be open to question, since the decision to ask this question rather than that, to view this behaviour as worthy of measurement rather than another must, in the final analysis, depend upon an act of judgement. Furthermore, there are great dangers in assuming that just because one measure of behaviour (representing, say, a certain style of teaching) correlates well with another (say, the child's score in a reading test), that there is a particular causal relationship between the two.

But it is not these difficulties which present the biggest obstacle to any attempt to give an objective account of how children learn in the classroom. Any explanation of the learning process must concern itself with the children's intentions, their interpretations and the thinking they bring to bear upon their activities. It is difficult to conceive of any device which could measure these things, correlate them with other factors and thereby provide the kind of objective results which so many educational researchers have sought.

No, in order to understand children's understanding we must first gain access to it. This cannot be achieved by the researcher who is separated from the children both physically and psychologically by the research tools used to measure their behaviour. But as teachers, on the other hand, with our close involvement with children and our professional skills which are intended to enhance our understanding of them, we are in a privileged position. The inner thoughts and intentions of the children will never be quite open to us and must always be inferred. But we are nevertheless in a position to relate closely to the children, to prompt their thinking and thereby to begin to reveal it, and so it is up to us to make the most of this privilege in order to gain insight into how our children learn and how we can best influence their learning.

This role for the teacher in educational research was suggested by Professor Hawkins.

> The transitions and transformations of intellectual development may be rapid indeed, but they are statistically rare and must be observed in context to be given significance. The most important area of control, for making the intellectual development of children more visible, happens to coincide with the major practical aim of educational reform: to provide both the material and social environment, and the adult guidance, under which the engagement of children with their world is most intrinsically satisfying and most conducive to the development we would study. Thus to be the best

scientific observers we must be at once the best providers for and the best teachers of those whom we would study.[3]

But underlying Hawkins' claim that we should somehow put together the roles of 'scientific observer' (or 'classroom enquirer' as I would prefer it in this context) and teacher, there lies a certain view of the teaching and learning relationship. Since such a view, or some germinal idea of it, predates the understanding represented in this present study, was developed by it, and underlies the kind of interpretations and selections I made while working with the children in the classroom, it is important to attempt at least to sketch it out here.

At the risk of oversimplifying a highly complex and philosophical matter, there appear to be two broadly different approaches to teaching which I shall call the transmission mode and the interpretative mode. According to the transmission mode of teaching, the teacher is seen as having, or having access to, certain knowledge and skills and as having the responsibility of transmitting these to the learner. Teaching proceeds according to objectives which, in principle at least, are predetermined by the teacher for any particular teaching period. The effectiveness of the teaching and learning can then be judged by the extent to which these objectives are met, that is, the desired knowledge and skills have been successfully transmitted. Characteristically, this mode of teaching concerns itself not so much with the processes by which children learn, but with the products of that learning, and indeed only those products which relate directly to the predetermined teaching objectives. With its emphasis upon the predetermined products of teaching, this form of learning is, on the face of it, testable. It is an approach to teaching and learning which fits well with an educational system which is concerned to sort and grade children through various levels of public examination.

But, to return to Hawkins' suggestion that an investigation of the learning processes can be incorporated into the role of the teacher, the transmission mode of teaching offers the classroom enquirer little access into how that process takes place. If our prime concern, in evaluating our teaching, is to examine the extent to which our predetermined objectives have been met, then there is a severe danger that we shall fail to see how the children understand, especially where their understanding is not in line with those objectives. On so many occasions during this present study, I was taken aback by the way in which a child had understood a situation totally differently from how I would have expected (see, for example, Dean's attempts to classify caterpillars, p. 26). In such instances the child's understanding, and my own insight into it, could only be developed given a relative freedom from too tight a set of teaching objectives.

The approach to teaching which played an increasing, though not exclusive, part in my own classroom practice prior to this study, and is, I would argue, an important element in any teacher's classroom enquiry into the nature and processes of children's learning, is an interpretative mode. While objectives play an important part in how the teacher provides resources and offers experience, skills and knowledge to the children, the act of teaching is not seen as being determined or evaluated only in terms of those objectives. According to this mode, the process of teaching and learning is two-way. It involves not only the child's attempt to interpret and assimilate the knowledge and skills offered by the teacher, but also the teacher's attempt to understand the child's growing understandings of the world. This concern to understand the children is not merely an attempt to evaluate whether or not a teaching objective has been successful (as in the 'examination'), but is a fundamental aspect of the interaction that takes place between teacher and learner as they learn together. The meaning of the knowledge, skills and experience involved in any teaching/learning act is not defined by the teacher alone, but is open to a process of reinterpretation as the children attempt to relate the experience afforded them to their existing knowledge. It is through such processes of reinterpretation, as teachers and learners strive to understand each other, that we gain some access and insight into the children's understanding. It is in this way also that we can evaluate the effects of our teaching.[4]

This interpretative mode of teaching places considerable emphasis upon the autonomy of the children. The choices they make and the ways they interpret the resources of the classroom are significant indicators to us of their understanding. To allow insufficient exercise of choice, or to inhibit the idiosyncracy of their interpretation, may not only close off possible avenues of their learning, but will also close our access to that learning. For this reason it was important, in this present enquiry, that I should be able to work with the children in a way which respected their autonomy.

From my experience of working on my own in a classroom, I had begun to realize that whenever I looked really closely at what the children were doing, the choices they were making and the forms of expression they were using, then a picture began to build up of a child who was, in some sense, more 'rational' than I had previously recognized. It seemed that, the closer I looked, not only the more I saw, but the more intelligent was what I saw. I had read so much educational writing that stressed the limitations of children's skill, knowledge and experience. What increasingly impressed me was that given these limitations, an interpretative mode of teaching reveals children to be making appropriate sense of their world.

Of course, with a class of thirty or so children one cannot always be relating to individuals or groups of children in a sufficiently close manner to gain this kind of optimistic insight. Nevertheless, it was those occasions when I was able to reflect sufficiently to provide some understanding of why the children worked in the way they did, that motivated me as a teacher. A few such insights into their learning were worth more than a battery of objective measures of their performance.

It was with this sense of optimism, combined with a desire to find out more about the children I taught, that I welcomed the opportunity offered when Michael Armstrong, another teacher, came to join me in my classroom for a year. His purpose in joining me was to combine the roles of teacher and researcher and thereby to investigate the quality of children's intellectual understanding and its growth. This enquiry, in which I became increasingly involved, is reported in his book, *Closely Observed Children* (1980). Subtitled 'The Diary of a Primary Classroom', the book follows and analyzes the painting, writings and explorations of a number of the children in my class. The year we spent together in 1976–77 turned out to be the first phase of a continuing programme of classroom enquiries of which this present study represents the second.

Hawkins had suggested that the roles of teaching and classroom enquiry could be combined. Now with two teachers teaching and enquiring together, it was possible to find the time and the space to sustain both. Furthermore, it soon became clear to me that two teachers with certain shared values are able to engage in a deeper analysis of the children's work than would be possible through solitary reflection.

The main theme that Michael Armstrong developed during that year was the concept of appropriation, the idea that 'from their earliest acquaintance with the various traditions of human thought, with literature, art, mathematics, science and the like, [children] struggle to make use of these traditions, of the constraints which they impose as well as the opportunities which they present, to examine, extend and express in a fitting form their own experience and understanding.'[5] Furthermore, his evidence suggested that 'intellectual growth can properly be seen as a product or consequence, of children's successive attempts at appropriation from task to task over the course of weeks, months and years.'[6]

These ideas, which were embodied in Michael Armstrong's descriptions of the children's work, tended to confirm my optimistic view of the child's intellect. However, I was concerned to develop

5

them in several ways. First, could the same claims be made of children working in a different classroom? Second, could this theme itself be developed by a further classroom enquiry? And perhaps of foremost importance to me was the role of the teacher in this kind of learning. If children can appropriate knowledge, what does this imply about the relationship between the learner and the teacher? An act of appropriation seems to suggest an attempt to control. In what sense can children take control of their own learning, and where does the teacher fit into this?

As I have suggested, a certain degree of autonomy, and hence the possibility and even desirability of children exercising some control over their activity, appeared to be an assumption upon which an interpretative mode of teaching and this kind of classroom enquiry were based. Some clearer understanding of what this autonomy amounted to, and how children could make use of it, would serve to develop my own approach to teaching. I also hoped that it might shed some light upon a recurrent and somewhat confused debate between so-called 'progressive' and 'traditional' approaches to teaching.

It was with this range of questions in mind that I embarked on the second phase of our programme of enquiry. For this, I gained the support of Leicestershire Education Department and Leicester University, to whom I was seconded for a research degree, to conduct fieldwork alongside another teacher in a different school. I was to spend a year in the classroom teaching and analyzing the children's work, followed by a year to write up my report (in the form of a research thesis) and prepare further developments in the programme. But before fieldwork began I taught for a year in the 'normal' situation of one teacher to thirty children. This year of 'normal' teaching persuaded me that while much more could be achieved with two teachers than with one, nevertheless the ideas which Michael and I had developed together were equally applicable in the less favourable circumstances.

In looking for a classroom and a 'host' teacher with whom to conduct this second phase of the enquiry, it was important that certain conditions should be met. Obviously, it was vital that the host teacher should appreciate the general purpose of the enquiry and be prepared to join in the analysis of the children's work. I would have to be relatively free from the day-to-day pressures of classroom organization so that time could be spent interacting closely with the children. Furthermore, it was important that the style of teaching in the classroom should be sufficiently open to encourage the children to make choices and to come to their own interpretations of the work. In other words, since the enquiry was intended to investigate the learning associated with an interpretative mode of teaching, such a way of working should be characteristic of the host teacher's style.

For, although I would not be attempting to subject the host teacher's teaching to critical scrutiny — inasmuch as teaching was an object of the study, it was my own teaching rather than the host's — any great divergence in our approaches could have caused unfortunate confusion amongst the children.

After visits to several primary schools in Leicestershire, I settled on a class of thirty-three 9 to 11-year-olds at Merton Primary School, Syston. Chris Harris, the class teacher, was the Deputy Head. There were eleven other class teachers and about 300 children housed in the 'open-plan' school with two mobile classrooms adjacent to the main school building.

The catchment area of the school consisted almost exclusively of a modern housing estate on the edge of the village of Syston. It is about six miles from Leicester where many of the children's parents worked. The houses on the estate were relatively inexpensive and appeared to be occupied largely by first-time buyers with young families and those who had moved from older terraced accommodation in Leicester. The socio-economic groupings represented in the intake of children therefore tended not to reflect the upper or lowest groups. The children were almost exclusively white and English speaking.

The headteacher, Stuart Ball, together with Chris Harris, encouraged an informal atmosphere and approach to teaching throughout the school. Chris worked with his class in an open area occupied by three other teachers and their classes which spanned the whole junior age range (from 7 to 11). Although the space was somewhat cramped, the teachers in this area made use of the open plan arrangement in the flexibility and cooperation it offered in the use of resources, timetabling and the setting up of occasional shared 'workshops'. Broad and integrated themes were adopted by the teachers in the area in consultation with each other. These themes provided a focus for much of the classroom activity but the individual teachers interpreted them in their own ways with regard for the needs of their particular children. Within the open area teaching was organized on a 'co-operative' rather than 'team' basis. Thus the children would feel free to approach other teachers for assistance but looked to their class teacher as having responsibility for guiding and developing all the central aspects of their work.

In the class in which I worked, Chris Harris allowed the children a considerable degree of autonomy in the direction of their work and the interpretations which they gave to his suggestions and stimuli. Apart from the mathematics and reading schemes which were used throughout the school, he made little use of commercially produced schemes of work, preferring to develop his own materials in response to the perceived interests and needs of the children.

From the beginning of the year we worked as a team in the classroom, both teaching most of the time. However, Chris Harris took responsibility for the overall management of the class, its curriculum, normal assessment procedures and so forth. This left me free, during class sessions, to focus my attention on individuals or groups of children for considerable lengths of time.

While the children naturally viewed Chris as their principal teacher, our activities in the classroom were almost indistinguishable. The children saw me as a second teacher, but soon began to ask questions concerning my role. All these I attempted to answer clearly and openly without providing such information unless requested. Gradually, several of the children developed a very good idea of the nature of my work and this proved helpful since they would often draw my attention to anything they thought would interest me. They knew that I would write about some of their work every evening, often taking samples of it home to examine more closely. These writings, or fieldnotes, in which I would record detailed observations and make interpretations of the children's work were, on occasions, made available to the children. It was often important that I should refer back to the children concerning an interpretation I had made of their work.

As the year progressed it became increasingly apparent that techniques I was developing primarily for the purposes of classroom enquiry were also useful aids to teaching. This tended to confirm my view of the essential integration of teaching and enquiry. For example, while I worked with children I would take many rough notes to record snatches of conversation, developments in the child's activity, or observational details that might otherwise have been forgotten when it came to writing up my fieldnotes at the end of the day. I would often discuss the children's work with the aid of these notes in order to review with them what they had done. Apart from providing an opportunity for the children to check the accuracy of my observations, these occasions enabled them to reflect upon their own work in a way which was most valuable. In fact, as will become evident in the following chapters, it was this propensity to reflect upon their work which proved to be such an important factor in their own learning.

In my fieldnotes, which averaged about 1000 words a day, I aimed not so much to give an overall impression of the classroom, or even a child's day within it, but rather to describe and interpret in detail an activity of one or two or perhaps a small group of children with whom I had been closely involved, or whose work seemed to be particularly interesting. At times I would play a major role in stimulating this activity by providing materials, making suggestions or raising questions, but often my involvement was the result of the children asking me to join them in something they were doing, perhaps following a suggestion from Chris Harris, or else working on an idea of their own.

In this way my notes followed no predetermined structure, being influenced more by the children's developing interest and our teaching concerns than by specific 'research' criteria. For this reason, it became vital to provide a retrospective structure to the material I was collecting. The notes were continually sorted, categorized and resorted in order to establish links between them, develop hypotheses about the children's learning, and identify areas in which more evidence was required. While I had approached the enquiry with a set of tentative ideas that resulted from my work with Michael Armstrong, it was important that my own observations should be informed, though not limited by, those ideas. My intention in allowing my fieldnote writing to be responsive to my varying day-to-day encounters with the children, but at the same time subjecting these notes to a continual process of categorization and re-analysis, was to ensure that, to a large extent, the theoretical ideas I was developing were grounded in the broad range of the children's classroom learning.[7] Without such discipline, there is a danger that classroom enquiry will result in no more than a confirmation of one's own presumptions. But this raises deeper questions which are better left to the final chapter of this book.

Every week Chris Harris would read my notes, comment on them and occasionally make his own notes concerning activities in which he had become involved. Stuart Ball would also read the notes regularly, and on occasions other members of staff were drawn in to discussion of the work. I would also show the notes to Michael Armstrong, who by now had his own class in the school where we had worked together, and our discussions would help me to relate the emerging ideas to those we had developed together in my classroom. Professor Simon, from Leicester University, who acted as a supervisor to my research degree, took a valuable interest in the fieldnotes and research thesis which resulted from them. In addition, a group of practising teachers from local schools met monthly in order to review the analyses that I was making and Michael Armstrong had made.

This broad range of discussion proved to play a vital part in the development of my ideas by applying alternative perspectives to them. But it was only later that I realized that it raised all kinds of questions about how teachers can conduct their own enquiries, how these can be shared and, in general, how we can learn from each other; more questions which I shall take up in the concluding chapter.

It is a difficult task trying to retrace the roots of one's own ideas and understanding, perhaps no less speculative than our attempts to follow the growth of ideas in children. The ways in which we make sense of the actions of others are inextricably linked to the ways in which we see ourselves. For this reason, the process of reflecting upon children's understanding inevitably involves an element of introspection, a conscious attempt to perceive not only how the child views the world — a world of literature, mathematics, art or play — but how we perceive this world too. This became clear to me as I wrote, for example, about the children's imaginative writing. For as I began to see how their fantasies were part of an attempt to make sense of their reality, so I gained a revitalized appreciation of the literature of the adult world. The classroom enquiry was, I felt, not only enabling me to teach more effectively, but also to learn more effectively.

The next two chapters consider, through examples of their activity, how children can relate to their teacher and their material environment in ways which enable them to exert an element of control over both. Chapters 4, 5 and 6 discuss the implications of this attempt to control on their abstract thinking, their writing and the growth of their skill. Chapter 7, a mini-case study, follows the development of a highly specific skill in one child over half a term, as an illustration of how some of the argument of the earlier chapters can apply in a single instance. The final chapter draws together the main themes of the book, gives an account of how this kind of enquiry has been extended to a wider range of teachers, and provides pointers for further classroom enquiry and its significance for practising teachers.

Notes

1 For example, BENNETT (1976), in *Teaching Styles and Pupil Progress*, considered that judgments made concerning children's creative writing were assumed to gain reliability by being marked by a panel of judges (see pp. 117–18). This is a confusion between consensus and reliability of judgment, concepts which are quite different when we are considering qualitative rather than quantitative aspect of analysis.
2 See, for example, Flanders' Interaction Analysis Categories in FLANDERS, N. (1970) *Analyzing Teacher Behaviour*, p. 34.
3 HAWKINS, D. (1974) *The Informed Vision: Essays on Learning and Human Nature*, p. 45, quoted in ARMSTRONG, M. (1980) *Closely Observed Children*, p. 4.
4 See JACKSON, P.W. (1968) *Life in Classrooms*, Ch. 4. There he finds that good primary school teachers do in fact evaluate the children's learning from the minute to minute flow of information between teacher and children, rather than from objective measures.
5 *Ibid.*, p. 129.
6 *Ibid.*, p. 131.

7 My approach here is described in detail in ROWLAND, S., *Enquiry Into Classroom Learning*, unpublished MEd thesis, Leicester University, 1980. It is an adaptation of the methods described in GLASER, B.G. and STRAUSS, A.L. (1967) *The Discovery of Grounded Theory: Strategies for Qualitative Research.*

Chapter 2

Relating to Children

Many writers and teachers have stressed the value of play. Working with Chris Harris and his children, it soon became clear to me that the recognition of this value underlay many of the activities in his classroom. Michael Armstrong, in his accounts of play-like activities in my own classroom two years earlier, had described how play can be an essentially intellectual activity.[1] What interested me now was how the children structured their play. Perhaps this would tell us something about the relationships we, as teachers, should try to develop with children.

To pursue this idea, I shall introduce Paula and Carol and some of their model-making. Paula and Carol, both 10 years old, had just returned from a short chat session with Chris Harris in which he had introduced the theme 'school' as an idea for the children to develop their own activities around. As I wrote in my notes that evening:

Fieldnotes: 9 October (Monday)
Carol and Paula wondered what it would be like if the school had not been built. What would the site of the school then have been used for? They suggested that it might be a campsite. Later they explained to me how there would be many tents where, on a fine night, children could come to sleep. Paula suggested that they would have to pay £1 a night to come and use the tents. She said there would also be a 'manager' who would live in the house alongside the camp site.

Carol and Paula had not been involved with some other children who had made various frameworks using drinking straws and pipe-cleaners the previous day. They had not seen the tent Jason had made using this technique, though they had seen one or two of the other structures. Paula's idea was that they could make tents by covering with tissue paper frameworks constructed out of drinking straws joined together with small pieces of pipe-cleaner.

By the time I came to watch them they had already made several tents. Some were based upon cubes, others upon long cuboids, others on square pyramids and there were various constructions of ridge tents.

Each tent was covered with tissue paper, stuck down with glue, with entrances left open where required. They explained how some small cuboid tents were to be 'loos', a large cubic tent was an 'entertainments tent' and the others were for sleeping. Another ridge tent they made but rejected saying that it was too large for their model. 'Look, it's even larger than the loos', Paula said. They felt that their ridge tents for sleeping in should be smaller than the 'loo' tents....

While Carol was experimenting with w.c. bowls for the 'loo' tents, Paula was constructing 'The Manager's House'. This was to be a cuboid with a roof of trapezium cross section.

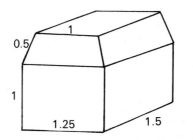

Numbers are lengths of members. Unit is one drinking straw.

Paula worked confidently at this, measuring up each member against another of corresponding length, before jointing it into the structure. When she had finished the framework, she stood it up on the table. It stood firmly enough but was a bit lopsided. She examined it and explained how this would be put right by shortening one of the roof gable members. She quickly cut a bit off this straw and, after reassembling, the house stood upright. I was surprised how well this repair job had worked, but pointed out to her that while the house stood quite upright and firmly, now one of the roof members was shorter than its corresponding members. Paula replied that she didn't think we needed to be that fussy and that, while it wasn't quite right, it would do. I agreed.

Carol, having finished her 'loos', told me how their campsite should have an adventure playground. For this she would make a climbing frame like the one in the school playground. She went out on her own to examine this, but made no sketches. She soon returned and started to build. First she made a cubic framework and then a lattice on one of its faces as shown here.

She explained to me: 'It's really a cube. You put two bits down like this (pointing to AC and BD) and then you cut out this bit (CD).' She explained how this lattice on the front face was repeated in a vertical plane down from GH, EF and JK. It was

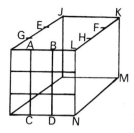

also the same, she said, on the face LKMN and its opposite face. (I later inspected the climbing frame in the playground more closely and, except for one small detail, her representation of it is quite correct.) It seemed extraordinary that she was able to analyze the structure in such detail and keep the information in her mind. Could she have done this before she had started working on the tent frameworks? I should guess that her work so far had given her some insight, increased her conception and perception of the geometry of frameworks. What had perhaps, earlier, been seen as a mass of horizontal and vertical bars, was now seen as a cube together with its sub-divisions and missing elements. While one cannot be certain, this seems the most plausible explanation for her considerable insight and ability to remember the details of the structure. Just as, by representing our thoughts and feelings in words, we are more clearly to understand them, so by modelling, Carol increases her understanding of the spatial configurations which she represents. . . .

The following school day Paula and Carol continued to model the seats, lamp-posts, fountains, cash desk and till, telephone booth and other features of the campsite. The objects were then mounted on a piece of stiff cardboard (about 1m by 1.5m) and carefully arranged with pathways between the tents and so on.

The display is now very impressive. The light shines through the orange tissue paper of the restaurant tent onto the little tables (made of pipe-cleaners, plasticine and plastic lid) which are set out with minute silver paper knives and forks, candles and cardboard glasses. In the entertainments tent their favourite pop star (pipe-cleaners) performs into a microphone. Behind these tents were the 'Ladies' and 'Gents'. The climbing frame had been adapted so that it could have ropes hanging down from the central section. Near this is the telephone booth and, at the other end of the board is the cluster of sleeping tents, paddling pool (a rectangle of silver card) and fountains. Lamp-posts stand amongst the tents.

Paula said that their model was 'Paradise'. But after discussing it amongst themselves they decided not to call it Paradise Camp Site. Laraine (who had now joined to help them) had said,

'It's going to be Luxury here' and they finally decided to call it 'Mount Posh'. Thus the little sign in front of the model which says, 'Welcome to Mount Posh'. . . .

Now that all the individual items are assembled it looks not only charming but surprisingly realistic. Their attention to scale has been precise throughout. They have also used considerable ingenuity in overcoming difficulties as they arose. For example, the restaurant tables could not be supported by the thin straws alone, so each straw had been reinforced by inserting a pipe-cleaner down its length. . . .

My intervention throughout this work was minimal. The two original ideas — the technique of jointing drinking straws with pipe-cleaners and the School Theme — had been provided by Chris Harris and myself but in different contexts and on different days. Neither of us had envisaged that they would be combined in this or any other way. Carol and Paula chose to respond to these two separate ideas by using them to construct what turned out to be their own fantasy world. Within such a world and the process of its construction I, as a teacher, played no significant part. While the girls were only too happy to talk to me about what they had done, my assistance (except in a few matters of material provisioning) was not required. This was not because the task they had set themselves was easy — on the contrary, it presented many considerable challenges — but because within their 'Paradise' they were the final arbiters upon whose judgments the value of the work depended. I was at best merely a sympathetic and interested outsider. This independence from my judgments was clearly demonstrated by Paula insisting that my criticism of her house was inappropriate: 'we needn't be that fussy.' From the delicacy and ingenuity of her constructions and her concern for such aspects as scale, it is clear that such a rejection of my tentative criticism was not merely a reflection of a lack of precision in her working style.

Their work was thus 'their own' in the broadest sense. Their control over its purposes and methods was ultimate. When, at one point, we discussed the names of the various shapes they had made (cube, cuboid, prism, trapezium, etc.) they were fascinated to learn them as applied to their shapes, shapes which had now become part of their everyday and imaginary experience. During the process of their work they needed to conceive of geometrical abstractions. There is little doubt that their ability to do this developed in response to the needs of the present task. No one had designed the task in order to develop these specific skills. When I had introduced the technique of making jointed frameworks to some other children the previous day, I did have in mind that spatial ideas might emerge. But no one had suggested that Carol or Paula should use this technique and they had not been present when I demonstrated it.

Was this development just a matter of good luck? Clearly some play-like activities are more productive of significant learning than others. I am not presenting the work of Paula and Carol as part of a claim that all play is educationally significant, or even that play should form a major part of the activity of a class of 9–11-year-olds, but simply that some play, of which this was an example, clearly enabled considerable learning to take place within a situation in which the children had complete control over their activity and in which the involvement of any adult was minimal. There were, no doubt, many types of learning associated with this particular activity, stemming from the social context and its imaginative and representational aspects, but what struck me most forcibly here was their development of spatial awareness: how they learned the names of several geometric shapes, investigated certain of their properties and increased their understanding of three-dimensional space.

The structure of this learning activity may be represented like this:

1 Children select   Children set   They develop specific
   stimuli to which → task   → concepts/skills
   they respond   required by the task

We may contrast such a scheme with one which describes practical activities which are structured by the teacher. For then the teacher decides upon certain specific concepts or skills which he feels require development; a practical task is set such that the children encounter or practice these skills or concepts; the child performs the task and thus acquires the required learning. This may be represented:

2 Teacher decides   Teacher designs/   Child   Child
   skills/   → sets appropriate → performs → acquires
   concepts   task   task   specified
                                                   learning

Scheme 1 above may be characterized as 'natural' learning, or learning which results from the children following 'the impulses inherent in childhood itself', to use Piaget's words.[2] The links between the stages take place naturally and there is no question of the appropriateness of the skills/concepts to their activity. Nor is there any question of interpretation of the task or of its interest value. Once the sequence has begun it is limited only by the extent of the children's present experience and knowledge, but it serves to extend both.

On the other hand, an activity which follows scheme 2 may be limited by:

a   the appropriateness of the decision to teach these specific concepts/skills to the stage of development, experience and interests of the child;

b   the appropriateness of these concepts/skills in terms of the curriculum;

c   the design of the task set: its suitability for furthering these particular skills/concepts;

d   the possibility that the child will not interpret and internalize the nature of the task as the teacher intended.

This second scheme is the basis for most curriculum design and much activity planning. Its success depends upon a high level of diagnosis of the individual children, knowledge of the subject matter and its relationship to the curriculum and to child development, ability to design or select appropriate tasks and to communicate them unambiguously. Attempts have been made to overcome these difficulties, or rather to bypass them, by programmed learning. But such techniques are appropriate only to skills and concepts which can be precisely defined and even then they tend not to stimulate their application to activities outside the structural course itself (that is, there is the problem of transferrence).

But scheme 1 also has its problems. We cannot leave learning merely to the chance responses of the children to their environment. Even if they frequently do learn in this way there remains the problem not only of providing a stimulating environment but also of ensuring that they develop a comprehensive range of skills and knowledge. This requires us to be more than merely provisioners of the learning environment.

I am not suggesting that classroom learning should follow the first 'play' scheme rather than the second 'teacher-structured' one, but that, in our relationships with the children and their work, we must be ready to exploit their natural tendency to learn, a tendency which was demonstrated in much of the play in Chris Harris's class.

An essential feature of play-like activity, which is usually lacking in the 'teacher-structured' approach, is the degree of control which the children are able to exert over their activity, By 'control', I do not mean only autonomy in the choice of the activity but also in respect of interpretations made in its course, its further development and overall objectives. Time and again it became clear to us that when the children exercised control, their activities developed rationally in response to events as they arose, while they bore in mind certain overall objectives. In this way, the children's exercise of control involved a structuring to their activity. In the work of Carol and Paula, this structuring took place without significant intervention on the part of Chris Harris or myself. But often conversations I had with the children played a more important role in enabling them to maintain control and develop the structure of their activity. It is this aspect of conversation that I now want to consider in more detail.

Julie and Louise, like many children of their age (10), enjoy making plays and have considerable talent in this field. Normally they chose to rehearse at home or in a quiet corner away from other children and teachers. We often saw their finished performances but on only one occasion was I involved in the process of its development. While their activity may be thought of as 'play' in some senses, my involvement in it was considerable. We talked a lot throughout the work, but I was always aware that while they valued our conversation, they did not need me to tell them what play acting was about.

Fieldnotes: 27 April
We went to the library where it was quiet and talked more about writing and acting. They decided they would like to act, by improvising a scene, with a view to discussing it afterwards. Before starting their acting they talked of rules that needed to be obeyed when they improvised. I was not sure what kind of rules they had in mind, and don't think they were altogether clear either, but they tried to explain: while acting they should not both speak at the same time; in the dialogue they should answer each other's questions and they should stick to the subject. Louise explained that without such rules it would be unrealistic and the conversation would be 'all over the place'. In a later discussion of rules she explained that in this scene she would have to be strict, that is, to keep in character with the strict mother whose part she was playing.

They were ready to start their improvising, but did not have any ideas for a subject for the scene so they asked me to provide one. I suggested a man returning from his work on night shift, expecting a meal from his wife who had been kept awake all night by their screaming baby. They improvised in a lively, if exaggerated, way for five minutes or so. Afterwards I asked them if they were aware of having kept to any rules. They both said they had not, but perhaps they would need to in a different kind of scene. They were keen to try something different but again wanted me to provide the theme. I suggested a scene to involve two mothers who had just attended interviews with their children's teacher. At both of these interviews the teacher had told the parent that their child was always fighting with the other child. After the interviews the mothers bump into each other outside the school.

Without further discussion they began their improvisation. After some 'telling off' of their respective children, whom they imagined to have now rejoined them after the interviews with their teacher, the two mothers met. Their cool hostility soon gave way to violent argument as each mother blamed the other for the scraps that her child got into. They almost came to blows before dragging their respective children away. Once home the children were given cursory chastisement before being sent off to bed. Finally, each mother said, in a somewhat reflective tone and as a 'thinking aloud' aside, how they regretted having lost their temper since they had thus made fools of themselves.

In discussing their improvision, Louise said, 'We got too mad, really. It made it alright later since we both said, "I wish I hadn't lost my temper" and so on.' Julie agreed. It was not altogether clear to me whether they saw this as a fault in their acting or as a fault of the mothers whose parts they acted. It was by now the end of the day, but this point was clarified when we met to continue the work this morning. Julie then explained their criticism further: 'You wouldn't lose your temper with another adult like that, but you would take it out on the children.' A very perceptive point.

They then talked about writing out the scene — a possibility I had raised earlier. They explained that the advantages of a written script would be that 'you wouldn't get it wrong' and there would be no unrealistic gaps in the dialogue when either actor was thinking of what to say. The chief disadvantage, they said, would be that a script takes a long time to write and has then to be learnt.

To speed up the script writing, they decided that each would write down only what she would say. In this way they scripted the first scene in which the mothers reprimand their children for their bad behaviour. They then acted this (with imaginary children) before adjusting the script and continuing with the writing. . . .

Having written the script, they acted it out. After the first acting several words were changed in the script. Julie said: 'It sounds alright when you write it but not when you read it.' So they acted it again. . . .

Comparing the scripted to the improvised acting, Julie said the former was 'better because it was all shouting in the other one.' Louise thought it better because they were 'telling the children off and not the other parent. It was more like my mum and Julie's — though they're really the best of friends — they don't shout at each other. They only shout at their children. . . . .'

Louise and Julie went on to make further improvisations which we discussed. Louise concluded that improvising had one advantage; 'It's more exciting without the words. There's more suspense. You don't know what's going to happen next.' Julie said that if they were to perform a play she thought it better not to write it out, but Louise thought that they would need to if it were to be performed by more than just the two of them.

My involvement in this considerably affected the course of this work. It was I who provided the themes of the two situations which they acted. (But this was only on their specific request for me to do so.) I was also the first to suggest the possibility of writing a script and at several points I suggested we might talk about what they had done so far.

But it seems inappropriate to use the word 'instruction' or even 'intervention' to describe my part. Both words have connotations of deliberation and premeditation. My comments and questions were not directed towards encouraging the girls to think or behave in a particular way, nor did I think their work was going off course and needed definite guidance. My contribution was in response to the exploratory nature of the situation. Our interactions were essentially 'conversational' in the sense that neither party sought to dominate the other. Nonetheless, such a relationship is not one of equivalence. My role was distinctive. I encouraged them to stop, reflect and talk about what they were doing. While I was in one respect involved in their activity (through our conversations), I was in another respect outside it since I did not act. My role may be described as one of holding up a mirror in order to help them reflect upon their experience more than they might otherwise have done. It was as a sympathetic and involved outsider, an adult and thus of greater general experience and someone with some professional knowledge of children, that I was able to stimulate conversation which encouraged them to pause and reflect critically upon their activity. Such reflection led to an appropriate structuring of the activity. This structure started with their concern for rules of acting and the need for realism. It was further developed by their decision to write a script and the comparisons they made between improvisation and scripted acting. They then considered in some detail the nature of the social relationships involved and how dramatic conventions can be used to express them. While this structure was rational, it was in no way premeditated by myself or the children. It developed in response to their reflective and critical thoughts as expressed in our conversations about what they were doing. It was in respect of these that my role was that of an enabler.

While children's experience of instruction is usually conceived in relation to a teacher, a parent or other adult, it is widely accepted that they learn from each other. Usually, the way in which a child learns from a peer is not formally structured. They learn from each other by sharing experience, contributing in a cooperative task, or simply by talking together. However, it appears that children have considerable awareness of their own ability, at least as it is perceived by their teachers.[3] A child will often take on the role of 'instructor' towards another child, be it a younger sibling or a peer. Perhaps a pair of friends consists of one who is recognized as being good at maths, the other as being good at writing. Such friends will often respect each other's superior skills and appeal to each other for help where appropriate. The instruction which takes place within such relationships may be sympathetic and most successful. But if the children are working in an environment in which they are allowed little opportunity to exercise control over their own work, one in which the teacher reserves the sole right to the direction and criticism of the children's work, then the help children offer each other is likely to be directed towards 'getting the right answer' with little regard for the learning process itself.[4]

During my fieldwork there were many occasions when the children would instruct each other with considerable success. For example, David had initiated a sequence of work which involved making patterns by tesellating perspective drawings of cubes. Greg became drawn into this activity which took place some five weeks after the work with pipe-cleaners and straws that was discussed earlier, though neither David nor Greg had been directly involved in that work. In this brief extract from the notes, David's idea for teaching Greg how to draw solid shapes in perspective shows considerable insight (or intuition) into the nature of the problem and the means for overcoming it.

> *Fieldnotes*: 7 November
> ... When Greg had finished his cubic designs we talked about the possibility of drawing other three-dimensional shapes. He successfully drew a variety of cuboids in perspective. I then suggested we look at some wooden prisms and tetrahedra that were in the classroom. In the ensuing discussion it became clear that Greg did not have the same understanding of the work as David. He had 'learnt' the technique of drawing perspective cuboids but appeared not fully to understand it and was unable to apply his skill to drawing other solid shapes. To help him, David constructed a cubic framework using pipe-cleaners and straws, pointing out that the cubic drawings represented such frameworks. Following David's suggestion, Greg then constructed a tetrahedron out of more straws and pipe-cleaners and used this as a model for further drawings. Later Greg drew an accurate perspective drawing of a prism without the use of a model, clearly demonstrating that he had now grasped the idea that he had found to be so difficult....

At times whole activities would proceed with the children recognizing each other's expertise and accepting the roles of teacher and learner which alternated depending upon which particular skills were required at any one time. There was a striking example of this one morning when Helen and Julie remained in the studio after Chris Harris had taken a dance/drama session. Chris had left a record of a selection from the Peer Gynt Suite playing. Left alone in the studio, Helen and Julie improvised a dance which told their own story. We then talked together. . . .

Fieldnotes: 10 October

After the session I asked Julie and Helen how they had decided upon the story. 'We didn't talk about it, we just did it,' they said. Helen said that they did not need to talk about their dancing, at least until after they had practised it. She explained, 'The dance tells you what to do.'

From our conversation it then became clear that Julie had taken ballet lessons for some time. Helen had done a lot of dancing and acting informally, but she said that she did not want to be taught by a teacher. 'You learn much better without one,' she said. They did a lot of dancing and acting together at home. . . .

In the afternoon they asked me to go back to the studio with them so that they could show me what they had been practising during the lunch break.

First they performed the two dances I had seen previously: 'The Hall of the Mountain King' (their rendering of which they called 'The Devil') and 'Morning' ('The Romantic Story'). Helen told me how the story of the latter had developed since they danced it this morning. The young man was a magician's son who entranced the princess by giving her gifts which were magic. At first the princess (Helen) turns down these gifts. Helen continued: 'So he gets fed up and goes. I wanted to gain riches' so she accepts the gifts 'but then I realize that it is wrong going after riches.' The gifts she is offered are 'a drink to make me kinder, a piece of fur to make my skin soft, shoes to make my feet lighter and this ring as a crown to make my hair softer.'

They insisted on showing me what they has practised to the other tracks of the record, the next of which was 'The First Arabian Dance'. It was clear throughout this piece that Julie was teaching Helen to dance. Whenever Helen made a movement that Julie did not think was quite right she would lift a finger, shake her head or in some other way mime her intention and then demonstrate how it should be done. During the performance Carol came into the studio (which had been empty apart from us) and passed a note to Helen. She took it without pausing in her dance. She glanced at it and passed it to Julie who also read it quickly and then threw it aside. Carol had meanwhile left the room. The flow of the dance had not been impaired. When the dance was over, no mention was made of the note, they were too concerned to dance and talk about their work.

At the time I was not sure whether the dance was about a dancing lesson in which Julie taught Helen, or whether Julie was simply helping Helen with the steps. They explained that the former was the case and that the piece, which they called 'The Art of Dancing' represented a dance lesson.

They went on to dance to 'Anitra's Dance' and 'The Return of Peer Gynt', after each dance telling me the story which they put to it.

Throughout these two dances it was clear that, while it was no longer part of the plot, Julie was indeed teaching Helen to dance. Swift nods and glances indicated to Helen how her performance could be improved.

Later I asked Helen about this. Who really had the ideas and led the dance? She said, 'They're my ideas really. I leave the steps of the dancing to Julie. I do the play, she does the steps.' Julie agreed.

What seemed extraordinary is how this division of responsibility worked in practice. While practising, very few words were spoken, indeed none during the dancing itself, just a few exchanges between sequences of movement. The sense of discipline was intense. Julie intelligently accepts Helen's leadership over matters of story line, Helen accepts Julie's over matters of dance. I asked Helen whether this did not sometimes lead to arguments. 'No', she said, 'We never argue except very occasionally and then it's a real bust up.'

The striking feature of the way Helen and Julie learned from each other was the extent to which their deliberate instruction served the purposes of the activity itself. It did not take place in isolation so that the skills mastered could *then* be applied in some imaginative way. The need for it arose from the activity. It was made possible by the naturally collaborative relationship between them as 'teachers' or 'learners' and their enthusiasm for the subject matter.

The examples I have considered so far have one aspect in common. In each case the work was initiated by the children. They started with a 'good idea' and from that point their ultimate control over the activity was established. They each had a degree of expertise and considerable enthusiasm for what they were doing and so needed no stimulation or instruction from Chris Harris or myself. They were their own masters throughout and so there was little danger that my contributions would take the control out of their hands. Thus it was not surprising that learning ensued according to the 'natural' scheme 1 above (p. 17).

There were, of course, many occasions when Chris Harris or I would interact more decisively with the children. Often they would need more positive stimulation before embarking on a course of activity. At times it seemed necessary positively to encourage some specific type of learning, or confrontation with a particular area of knowledge, in order that the children should have the opportunity to develop a broad range of abilities. Perhaps the activities described so far present a paradigm of learning in which the children had control over the objectives and processes of their work. But could this control be maintained when I saw the need to act more decisively? Would not such decisive intervention take the control of the activity out of their hands? Could the relationship between us still maintain the sense of equality and conversationality? Or would this be where 'play' ends and 'work' begins?

Often when I took a more decisive role with the children in Chris Harris's class, they appeared able to maintain this element of control and it was important that they should do so. But such control was not of an exclusive nature. It did not exclude me but indeed required my support for it to be maintained. While teachers are not in all senses equal to the children in their investigations they will usually have greater experience and knowledge of the subject matter and a professional knowledge concerning children's learning — there can remain a sense of equality before subject matter within which they both collaborate and which is beyond them both. As David Hawkins puts it, 'Adults and children, like adults with each other, can associate well only in worthy interests and pursuits, only through a community of subject matter which extends beyond the circle of their intimacy.'[5]

Perhaps the essence of a conversation or of collaboration is the way in which both parties respect each other's interpretations. As long as children feel compelled to accept their teacher's interpretations and objectives they are likely to undervalue or even reject their own ideas where they do not conform to the teacher's, thus losing their control over the activity. The task for them will then become merely one of finding out what is in the teacher's mind and acting accordingly.

Often I would make suggestions during the course of an activity in the belief that my ideas would steer the child's explorations along a certain course, one which, for one reason or another, I thought to be appropriate. While these interventions often had considerable effect in changing the course of events, they were interpreted by the children in quite unexpected ways. Such reinterpretation was not necessarily the result of failure to communicate (although on occasions it is likely to have been), but it was the children's way of relating my contribution to their particular interests and objectives. They would often thereby reinterpret in a way which was not only more appropriate to their needs but which led to aspects of the subject matter being revealed which were important and had at first perhaps been overlooked by me.

An intriguing example of the critical reinterpretation of my suggestions occurred with Dean towards the end of the year. He, together with William and several other children, had spent some days collecting caterpillars, examining them, building vivaria, inventing experiments to test their ideas, drawing, writing and so on. At the time of this next extract Dean was sitting next to William at a table. While William drew, I worked closely with Dean who had just completed some writing about his creatures. Before us was a pot full of grass with various caterpillars crawling around inside it.

> *Fieldnotes*: 5 June
> ... We talked about species. We had not examined any reference books together and Dean did not seem concerned to find out the real names for the different varieties. Instead, he had invented his own names. A type of thin small caterpillar he called 'Mr. Diet'; the black and yellow ones were 'Arthur'; the brown furry ones 'Stannage'. He did not use these as 'pet' names but as names which referred to any caterpillar which appeared to be of that type.
>
> But as we watched William drawing a caterpillar a problem arose. William was carefully drawing a 'Cyril' which had six 'legs' and ten 'suckers'. Dean noticed that most of the ones he had called 'Cyril' only had six 'legs' and four 'suckers'. He didn't suggest inventing a new name for this different variety of 'Cyril'. Thinking that we should clarify our criteria for classification, I suggested that we list the different varieties we had in a table in which columns indicated the name, colour, number of 'legs', number of 'suckers' and comments relating to each variety of caterpillar.
>
> As we talked about my idea, Dean thought it was a good one. But when he began to fill in the table, he became frustrated about the differing numbers of 'legs' and 'suckers' on the various 'Cyrils'. He said, 'I call all green ones like that Cyril. I'm not bothered about how many legs they've got.'
>
> It seems that I had imposed my own system of classification and Dean did not like it.
>
> We then talked about how his caterpillars differed. I was now keen not to impose my own ideas and Dean decided that

these should be the attributes we should look for: colour; fat, thin or medium; hairy or not hairy; where it was found or what it ate (considered normally to be identical). He made a table like this:

Colour	Fatness	Hairy	Found on	Sameness
green	thin	not hairy	hawthorn	not the same
yellow and grey	fat	bit hairy	hawthorn	
brown	fat	hairy	dock leaf	not the same
brown	medium	bit hairy	hawthorn	

I asked him why he had headed another column 'sameness'. He said, 'So I can write down if they're the same or not.' My objection seemed to me to be too simple and obvious to explain. I had assumed that the purpose of such a table was to list the attributes of different classes of caterpillar. Dean, apparently, saw it as a way of recording the attributes of his different individual creatures. I did not explain my point except to say that I could not see the need for the last column. He explained that he would list all his caterpillars in pairs and say, for each pair, whether or not the caterpillars were identical. I said, 'But surely, if they are the same, you wouldn't bother to list them both?' He said that he would and that he would show me how when I returned to school tomorrow. There seems to be quite an exercise in logic in this.

One satisfaction of working with Dean (though at times a frustration too) is his willingness to reject or modify strategies that I suggest. In this business of classification I think that problems will be encountered by him following his own strategies which would have been glossed over had he merely followed mine. It will be interesting to see whether the problem still interests him tomorrow. He does appear so far to have wanted to work at a level of abstraction beyond what I might have expected.

Fieldnotes: 7 June
Yesterday Dean did want to return to making his table of comparison for his caterpillars. He got down to it as soon as he arrived, ten minutes or so before the official beginning of school. He selected two caterpillars to record and wrote in the columns:

green and black	thin	not hairy	hawthorn	not the
green, black and white	medium	not hairy	hawthorn	same

Before completing the final 'sameness' column he did not look at the insects to see if they in fact were of the same appearance, but instead checked through his columns, comparing entries, to establish that the entries were different. Thus the 'sameness' column did not refer directly to the appearance of the insects or whether, on some other evidence, he thought they were of the same type; but rather was an identity relationship between the attributes which he had selected to compare. This is a subtle, but I think most important, distinction since it shows the level of abstraction at which Dean was working.

Dean then went on to show me how he would record the entries of similar caterpillars. He first selected two individuals to record. He thus was not merely going to write down the same entry twice. Each entry had to correspond with observations made of a particular caterpillar. For each he completed the attribute columns: green and white; thin; not hairy; hawthorn. 'Same' was written against the entries in the 'sameness' column. Dean then put on a perplexed and frustrated expression, saying that he needed an extra column. He said this should be a 'name' column. I asked him if he meant a column for names like 'Cyril', 'Stannage' and 'Arthur' that he had invented. He said, 'No. It must be for their real names.'

Dean seemed to have discovered the need for a taxonomy. having selected (what he considered to be) criterion attributes by which to describe the caterpillars, he saw that a class could be made of those creatures with identical attributes, and that such a class should be given a name. It was this identity of selected attributes, rather than direct appearances, which characterized Dean's conception of class and is indeed central to any such system of classification. . . .

By this stage Dean was ready to make use of a reference book, from which he identified his last recorded caterpillar as being that of a Winter Moth.

There is little doubt that had Dean uncritically followed my original suggestion of tabulating his invented names for the caterpillars against my selection of attributes he would never have confronted the problems of classification and taxonomy in such depth. His approach may seem somewhat eccentric (and therefore unpredictable) to us, but then we take for granted, or perhaps have never enquired into, the internal logic of the problem with which Dean was concerned.

Dean's readiness to reinterpret my strategy for classifying his caterpillars may be viewed as an appropriate expression of a natural desire to make sense of his environment, to 'assimilate' it to himself and 'accommodate' himself to it, to use Piaget's terms. I shall consider this aspect in more detail in the next chapter, in relation to the material environment.

The ease with which the children were able to maintain control, or regain it, depended upon the strength and level of my intervention. Obviously, were I to have intervened in a very strong (authoritarian) way, insisting that such and such be done, then they would have been denied the opportunity of taking the initiative and would have been unlikely to gain control over their activity. But my understanding of the teacher/learner relationship so far, in general, ruled out such intervention as destructive to this relationship. On the other hand, a high level of intervention was necessary when I wished, either in response to a problem which had arisen during the course of an activity or as a stimulus to further activity, to offer the children a more formal, detailed or complex set of instructions. As far as the children were concerned, the problem then became one of regaining their control by reinterpreting and applying such ideas and techniques to a context that was meaningful to them. Detailed techniques, for example, often required some considerable practice by the children within a relevant context and under close supervision, before they were able to use them in a way which they could control. But if they were to regain this control, it was important that I should avoid continuing my direction of their work, since they were then likely to become dependent upon me. Surely, we should guide children into new paths towards knowledge, but avoid holding their hands too tightly for too long. Otherwise they may fail to assimilate such knowledge into their own experience.

This handing over of control presents problems. Often I have been anxious to ensure that all areas of the curriculum were covered, that certain 'standards' were achieved, and have felt that I could not afford to do this; that it would leave too much to chance. Even when external pressures were reduced to a minimum — as they were in this present enquiry — there were occasions when my own enthusiasm prevented me from handing control back to the children. More than once did I enter the classroom with 'exciting ideas' to 'get the children going' and they soon took on my enthusiasm in the new work. But then, as the work proceeded, it became increasingly clear that the children had built up a dependency upon me. While they were keen to follow and act upon my ideas, they seemed unable to conjure up any of their own. I became firmly established at the centre of the stage and could not withdraw to the wings without the show collapsing. At the end of such experiences I felt that it had been enjoyable but it had somehow got us nowhere. The question remained: and what next?

From this I would not wish to conclude that we should restrain our enthusiasm. Indeed, it should be infectious and inspire the kind of independent learning desired. The problem arises because of a failing in the relationship between the teacher, the learner, and the subject matter. The subject matter and engagement in it should extend 'beyond the circle of their intimacy', as Hawkins puts it. As long as it is not seen as our possession, as teachers; as long as we are not seen by the children (or ourselves) as having sole access to it; then we can be sensitive to the children's interpretations and reactions, value these and help them to develop their activity accordingly. Only then will they be able to regain control of the process of their own learning, while we become, as Bruner puts it, 'part of the student's internal dialogue.'[6] Later in the same book, he says, 'To isolate the major difficulty, then, I would say that while a body of knowledge is given life and direction by the conjectures and dilemmas that brought it into being and sustained its growth, pupils who are being taught often do not have a corresponding sense of conjecture and dilemma.'[7]

It was the opportunity for such conjecture and dilemma that proved to be the key to the children's retaining or gaining control over their activity. When this opportunity was offered the children were indeed able to make the most of it and strived to do so, in order to control their work. Whenever they said, 'I wonder what would happen if ...?' or 'How could this be so?' they had begun to define their problems, the essence of their control over their work.

In this next sequence of activity with David and Greg, I was clearly confronted with this problem of handing over control to them. I had been stimulated by some conversations with a mathematician, and my own reading, on aspects of the famous Fibonacci series, a series of numbers which has many strange properties. From the outset of my introducing some of these ideas to David and Greg, I was only too aware that, while there seemed to be unlimited potential here for us to explore, it would not be easy for me to hand over control to them. Certain techniques and approaches to constructing and analyzing the series needed to be followed if anything fruitful was to emerge. The problem seemed to be one of introducing such techniques in a way which did not then cast me in the role of the one who 'knows all the answers' and therefore force a dependence of the children upon me. In my enthusiasm for the investigations I also had to make a conscious effort to be receptive to what they thought about what we were doing and not to get carried away on my own path.

Fieldnotes: 12 October
... I started working with David and Greg, two friends who are interested in numbers though they have no particularly striking skills in formal aspects of arithmetic.
   I first explained the rule for forming a Fibonacci series.

Starting with the terms 1,1, each term is made by adding together the two previous terms:

1,1,2,3,5,8,13,21,34,55,89, ...

We made this series together and spent some time examining it, seeing how its terms grew. It soon became apparent to me that the arithmetic involved could be made much simpler by reducing each term to a single digit by adding the digits in its number (thus 13 becomes 4 and the eighth term would then be $8 + 4 \rightarrow 12 \rightarrow 3$). With Greg acting as scribe and David checking the calculations, they transformed the above Fibonacci Series into a Reduced Fibonacci Series:

1,1,2,3,5,8,4,3,7,1,8,9,8,8,7,6,4,1,5,6,2,8,1,9,1,1,2,3,

When they got this far they realized that the last four terms were the same as the first four and that the series was repeating itself.

David and Greg clearly needed some help with analyzing this series. I suggested that we count the number of terms in the first cycle of the series, cut the series into two halves (twelve terms in each half) and add together corresponding terms in each half. Like this:

1 1 2 3 5 8 4 3 7 1 8 9   8 8 7 6 4 1 5 6 2 8 1 9
First term in first half   + First term in second half $= 1 + 8 = 9$
Second term in first half + Second term in second half $= 1 + 8 = 9$
Third term in first half   + Third term in second half $= 2 + 7 = 9$

and so on, with the sum of each pair being 9.

None of us could explain why this 9 repeated itself, but David and Greg were obviously excited by the discovery. It seemed to me better at this stage to help them to find more such patterns before attempting to untangle the reasons for them.

Greg then suggested that we make another series the same way but starting with 2,2 instead of 1,1. He did this, with David watching and checking his figures. Again, he found that the series repeated itself after twenty-four terms.

The rest of the afternoon was spent constructing similar series starting with (3,3); (4,4) and so on up to (9,9). I suggested recording these series in the form of a matrix. Greg worked at this slowly and accurately. David left all the calculating to Greg, preferring to concentrate on picking out the various patterns which emerged.

At the end of the day they both decided to take home large sheets of squared paper on which to continue the work. Greg was going to write up the results so far. David would try to make up a new series.

The next morning David told me how he had 'got stuck'. In fact a small arithmetical error had thrown his series out. Greg had completed the matrix like this:

and so on

```
[1 1] 2 3 5 8 4 3 7 1 8 9 [8 8] 7 6 4 1 5 6 2 8 1 9 [1 1]  →
[2 2] 4 6 1 7 8 6 5 2 7 9 [7 7] 5 3 8 2 1 3 4 7 2 9 [2 2]  →
[3 3] 6 9 6 6 3 9 3 3 6 9 [6 6] 3 9 3 3 6 9 6 6 3 9 [3 3]  →
[4 4] 8 3 2 5 7 3 1 4 5 9 [5 5] 1 6 7 4 2 6 8 5 4 9 [4 4]  →
[5 5] 1 6 7 4 2 6 8 5 4 9 [4 4] 8 3 2 5 7 3 1 4 5 9 [5 5]  →
[6 6] 3 9 3 3 6 9 6 6 3 9 [3 3] 6 9 6 6 3 9 3 3 6 9 [6 6]  →
[7 7] 5 3 8 2 1 3 4 7 2 9 [2 2] 4 6 1 7 8 6 5 2 7 9 [7 7]  →
[8 8] 7 6 4 1 5 6 2 8 1 9 [1 1] 2 3 5 8 4 3 7 1 8 9 [8 8]  →
[9 9] 9 9 9 9 9 9 9 9 9 9 [9 9] 9 9 9 9 9 9 9 9 9 9 [9 9]  →
[✗ ✗] [1 1] 2 3 5 8 4 3 7 1 8 9 [8 8] 7 6 4 1 5 6 2 8 1 9 [1 1]  →
```

and underneath had written:

'The top and bottom row of our pattern both have exactly the same numbers because: 10 10 2 tens are wrong but 1 1 'two' 'ones' are right because we are only using Single Figured numbers. You may be amazed to see a whole line of nines this is because $9 + 9 = 18$ well $1 + 8 = 9$ you see 18 is $10 + 8$ and $10 + 8 = 18$.'

We had only talked briefly the previous day about the final 10,10, → 1,1, series. Note here that while Greg's style of writing is precise and logical, it is highly personal: 'You may be amazed to see . . . well . . . you see.' Though such comments are not part of the nature of a mathematical proof, here they appropriately demonstrate Greg's excitement and close identification with the ideas he expresses.

The 'boxed' numbers represent the pattern which David spotted yesterday. He also pointed out the column of third terms (2,4,6,8,1,3, . . .) explaining that this was really 'going up in twos, the 1 and 3 really meaning 10 and 12.' (They did not realize at this point that indeed every column is a 'times table,' reduced.) By now David, who had not done much in the way of calculating the previous day, decided to leave us so that he could work out for himself all the series we had made so far. I was surprised at his decision. I had expected him to avoid the hard work and only to get involved in the pattern spotting. But now he apparently realized that the activity had many possibilities and he would rather practise the appropriate technical skills before progressing further. So he went off without any of Greg's figures to do it all over again for himself. Only once or twice did he ask for my help after suspecting he had made a mistake because the patterns he had in mind were not coming out right.

So far Greg had been very much led by me in this work. He fully understood everything and worked out the calculations himself, but had not had any ideas of his own for further exploration. Hoping to encourage him to branch out more, I suggested that, if he wanted to make more series, he could either change the rule of construction (that is, replace the 'add two previous terms' rule of the Fibonacci Series by some other rule) or change the initial terms. He decided on the latter, and, using the same rule, started another Reduced Fibonacci Series with (1,2). He soon saw that his new series was merely the (1,1) series displaced by one term (1,2,3,5, ... instead of 1,1,2,3). Pleased by this, he started again with (2,3). Again he soon saw that this was the original (1,1) series, but this time displaced by two terms (2,3,5,8, ... instead of 1,1,2,3, ...). His next series he started with (3,4). This he completed until it began to repeat after twenty-four terms. Then the same starting with (4,5) until this also repeated after twenty-four terms.

We then looked closely at our original matrix of series. I pointed out that the numbers (3,4) appear adjacent to one another in the matrix as the eighth and ninth terms of the series beginning (7,7). Greg noticed that his new (3,4) series was merely a contination from that point in the (7,7) series. Similarly, we found that his new (4,5) series was a continuation from the tenth and eleventh terms of the (4,4) series in our matrix.

We then saw that our original matrix contained every possible combination of two digits adjacent to one another and thus that any Reduced Fibonacci Series starting with any two digits could be found within that matrix.

By now we were treading on ground quite new to both of us. I had not envisaged all this. Greg was enthralled. He said, 'It contains everything. It must be magic!'

Greg then said he would change the construction rule. 'I am now going to add on certain numbers. I don't think you'll understand that.' (Even in his chat, he is concerned that his meaning may not be quite clear). He then showed me what he meant. It would be a straightforward arithmetical progression starting with 2 and adding 2 for each term, reducing to single digits in the usual way. Thus:

2,4,6,8,1,3, ...

And saw, with amazement, that this also occurred in the

original matrix as the third column. (He had forgotten that David had pointed out this feature the previous day.)

He then made a similar progression in threes (3,6,9,3, ...) and saw that this corresponded to the fourth column of the matrix. He then saw that any such arithmetical series (or 'table') was represented in the columns of the matrix.

Then Greg said, 'I'm going to think of something that might not be here' (in the matrix). After some thought, he explained how he would make a series by adding the two previous terms and then adding 5 to this result. Thus after the two initial terms (5,5) the third would not be 1 (5 + 5 → 10 → 1) but 6 (1 + 5 → 6). Each term would be similarly increased by 5 after adding the two previous terms. He soon had written:

5,5,6,7,9,3,8,7,2,5,3,4,3,3,2,1,8,5,9,1,6 ..

and said, 'Come on. I want to see 5,5 again.' Sure enough, the series repeated as he had expected after twenty-four terms:

... 3,5,4, (5,5)

and, as Greg had intended, this series did not occur in his matrix.

Greg employed various strategies to further analyze this series, breaking it into halves, then quarters, adding corresponding terms and so on. This produced no further clear patterns. (Had Greg used exactly the same strategy as I had used in analyzing our first Reduced Fibonacci Series he would have found a repeating number.) But after various manipulations with the figures he ended up with four terms 8,2,4,1. I pointed out to him the doubling relationship between these terms and Greg said, 'Yes, double it! That's given me an idea', and proceeded to explain how a new rule for construction could be: double previous term and reduce to single figure (that is, a geometric progression).

He went off to work on his own and soon returned to show me what he had done.

```
3 6 3 6 3 6
1 2 4 8 7 5          (1 2 4 8 7 5)
2 4 8 7 5 1          (2 4 8 7      )
4 8 7 5 1 2          (4 8 7 5      )
5 (1 2 4 8 7 5 1)    (Note 5 and 1)
6 3 (6 3 6)          (Note 6 and 3)
7 5 1 2 4 8 (7 5)
```

His words 'Note' refer to the displaced identity between series starting with 5 and 1 and between those starting with 3 and

6. The brackets suggest the repeating nature of the series. When we examined these series together we saw that every series except those starting with either (3), (6) or (9) is identical except displaced. Greg pointed out that the doubling series starting with (9) would simply be 9,9,9, ... (that is, 9,18,36,72 ... → 9,9,9,9, ...). He then said the series starting with 10 would really be a series starting with 1.

He then said, 'If we were enormously clever we could triple them', that is, produce tripling geometric series.

He worked on his own while I watched. He completed this:

1 3 9 9 9 ... He saw that since 9 × 3 = 27 → 9
2 6 9 9 ... and 27 × 3 = 81 → 9, once 9 occurred
3 9^A 9 ... in the series, it would simply
4 3^B 9 ... continue to repeat itself.
5 6 9 ... When he had got as far as (A) he
6 9 9 ... said, referring to the second *column*
7 3 9 ... of the emerging matrix,
8 6 9 ... 'Look, it's 3,6,9, again', and at
9 9 9 ... (B) 'We're just going to start again'
(that is, the column will repeat itself).

Meanwhile David, working on his own, had completed the matrix of Reduced Fibonacci Series. It was near the end of the afternoon and he said, 'When I go home I'm going to make a new one.' He said he would start with (9,9) and use the rule of adding the two previous terms and also 2 to this sum (that is, similar to Greg's invented series which David had watched him make). He said, 'This is going to be easy, It'll just be: 9 9 2 2 2 ....' I asked him why. He said that since 9 + 9 → 18 and 18 + 2 → 20 → 2 the next term would be 2 which would just repeat itself. Suspecting his reasoning here, I suggested he do it now. He was keen to, and soon saw that his hypothesis was wrong as the series started: 9,9,2,4,8.... He said, 'You've gotta make mistakes. It'll go back to 9,9 anyway. I'll make it!' In spite of his mistake, he does not lack confidence and feels quite in control of the situation.

Sure enough, after twenty-four terms, David's series did start to repeat itself.

And so ended two days of arithmetic. David and Greg said they had enjoyed it very much. David had earlier shown some concern as to whether this would help them when they get to their secondary school next year. I said I thought it would. Thereupon they decided to spend three days a week doing this kind of maths'. 'We'd need a break sometimes', added Greg.

They did indeed go on to do much more work on this (though their decision to work on it three days a week was a little extravagant!). They went on to develop more series and explored ways of transforming them into straight line patterns.

No doubt much was gained by all three of us from this work. It certainly affected David and Greg's approach to arithmetic, now they saw numbers as 'beings' which had a certain mystique. This seems to be the underlying emotional response of the pure mathematician. The fact that the numbers did not count things did not mean that they were the meaningless abstractions which is often the case with 'sums'.

But throughout the first day of work, I was very much the performer and leader of the discoveries. While they did make their own series and spot patterns emerging, each development of the activity was initiated by myself. They were completely dependent upon me. This was demonstrated by the fact that the work Greg did at home after the first day was simply a repeat of what had been done with me. I do not mean to imply that it was therefore of no value, but that it demonstrates his inability or disinclination, in spite of considerable enthusiasm, to take the work further on his own.

On the second day, David's decision to go off on his own and practise the technique of building series is a clear indication of his desire to make the work his own, to control it and to reduce his dependency upon me (and Greg) in making the necessary calculations.

The point at which Greg really began to exercise his control in the work is clearly seen. In the middle of the second day, after we had made Reduced Fibonacci Series starting with every possible combination of two figures, I noted, 'By now we were treading on ground quite new to *both* of us.' And then, only two lines later: 'Greg then said he would change the construction rule.' From this point onwards the nature of the series investigated branched out considerably, no longer following the Fibonacci rule of construction. Greg proceeds to initiate a sequence of investigations, inventions and hypotheses based upon a now heightened awareness of what a series is and some good approaches to discovering its pattern-making potential.

Is it really a coincidence that Greg started to take the initiative in his enquiries at the very point at which I also felt that I was treading on new ground? It seems that the freshness of the discoveries for me cast me in a truly collaborative role, rather than in a primarily leading one in which I possessed all the clues to the progress of the work. From this point the investigations took on a sense of spontaneity similar to that of an art as characterized by Dewey: 'The spontaneous in art is complete absorption in subject matter that is fresh, the freshness of which holds and sustains the emotion.'[8]

Of course it would be unrealistic to suppose that each time we initiate an activity, or offer specific instruction or guidance, we can expect children to make discoveries which are in every sense new to us. Usually we shall have trodden the ground before they reach it. But there is a strong sense in which as soon as they begin to tackle real problems, problems as they have constructed or interpreted them, then learning takes places and the knowledge which is gained is not merely a copy of our knowledge, but is a reconstruction of it. Such knowledge may view the same objective world and concern itself with the same facts, but will offer a perspective upon them which is individual and to that extent unique and new.

In the last chapter I suggested that Michael Armstrong's concept of 'appropriation' seemed to imply that children control their learning in some way. The examples of work in this chapter, among many of those activities in Chris Harris's class where the children were really absorbed, illustrate how the children did in fact seek to exercise this control, but that it required a certain kind of relationship between teacher and child. This relationship is perhaps best understood as a kind of 'conversation' or 'collaboration'. It is from this perpective, as I attempted to become 'part of the student's internal dialogue', that the children's work in the next chapter should be viewed. Here I want to consider how the children developed purposes and intentions in response to the material environment of the classroom.

Notes

1 Armstrong, M. *op. cit.*, Ch. 6.
2 Piaget, J. (1969) *Science of Education and the Psychology of the Child*, p. 151.
3 See, for example, Nash, R. (1973) *Classrooms Observed*, in which he says: 'even children as young as eight gave themselves positions which correlated highly with those assigned them by the teachers.'
4 This observation is confirmed by the findings of Leicester University's ORACLE project in that interactions in the primary classroom between children and concerning their work are found to be of a largely didactic nature. See Galton, M. *et al.* (1980) *Inside the Primary Classroom*.
5 Hawkins, D. (1974) *The Informed Vision: Essays on Learning and Human Nature*, p. 49.
6 Bruner, J.S. (1966) *Toward a Theory of Instruction*, p. 124.
7 *Ibid.*, p. 159.
8 Dewey, J. (1934) *Art as Experience*, p. 70.

Chapter 3

The Material Environment

In Chris Harris's classroom, the children were confronted with a wide range of materials which were intended to stimulate them into activity, to encourage them to reflect upon their activity and the world around them, and thereby to develop their skill and knowledge. The materials were informally organized, and emphasis was placed upon the children's freedom to choose which materials to work with and to determine how such work should proceed. They were encouraged to use materials in an inventive way, and even when suggestions were made for their use, it was intended that they would explore and develop these ideas in an individual manner. On those occasions when the whole class or group of children were confronted with a specific range of experiences — such as on a field trip or in a maths group — considerable emphasis was placed upon diversity and individuality in how they developed their work.

In such 'open-ended' confrontations with the material environment the children's work is often perceived as being exploratory. Current trends in opinion view such activity with some degree of scepticism. For example, the HMI's (1978) report, *Primary Education in England*, characterizes an 'exploratory', as opposed to a 'didactic', approach as being one in which 'the broad objectives of the work were discussed with the children but where they were put in a position of finding their own solutions'.[1]

It is assumed that where children are working in such a way 'guidance and instruction will be lacking', a state of affairs which 'could lead to aimless activity and lack of progess'.[2] Such a description is inclined to ignore the collaborative and conversational aspects of the teacher's relationship with the child and the ways in which these operate in the process of the child's discoveries, features which were discussed in the previous chapter. The report also describes children as being 'put' into such situations, implying a passivity on their part which could appear to be inconsistent with the role of explorer. Exploratory activity becomes aimless when explorers are lost; when they are unable to interpret or make sense of the clues which the environment offers. In such activity they have lost control since they are now at the mercy of chance and mere fancy.

While Chris Harris and I attempted to stimulate a sense of exploration amongst the children, there were, of course, times when their enthusiasm was not immediately forthcoming. Often children would approach me in a state of indecision. At times like this they appeared to be 'fishing around' for ideas: searching for a stimulus to which they could respond. Such a state is not to be confused with boredom. Rather it is an active state, often of considerable sensitivity and expectation, but which has not yet found an object upon which to focus.

When we talked to children when they were in this state, a certain pattern seemed to emerge. Their attention was directed both inwards and outwards. Inwardly, they may have been thinking of the successful activities they had recently been involved in, their present interests, or perhaps they were recollecting some interest from the more distant past which could be taken up again, or some work which might now be completed. In general, such thoughts seemed to constitute a search for a loose end or a gap in their own experience which future activity might latch onto or fill. Outwardly, they reviewed the possibilities offered by the environment: perhaps the art area had some new paints, more books had been added to the class library, there was a large box of modelling 'junk' which had not recently been inspected, or perhaps we had introduced some theme or suggestion which might be taken up.

A role for myself as a helper in this process of reflection and weighing up the possibilities was apparent. But it was often the child who eventually decided on a particular course of action, having seen the link between the inward and the outward possibilities. The following example serves to explain what I mean by 'seeing the link'.

Ian would often discuss his plans for work with me. I usually helped him with his writing which he found very difficult. He was only just beginning to learn to read. Recently he had been involved in many drawing activities. Among these were plans of houses, maps and a series of lorries and battleships. The last were very fine in their way, being mostly carefully drawn with a ruler, but appeared to me to show little development, each ship being almost identical to the previous one. He had also been very interested in modelling, in particular with wood. When he approached me one afternoon, saying that he wanted to do something exciting and different, but that he did not know what, he soon began to tell me about his previous work. As if thinking aloud, he talked of the stories he had enjoyed writing, the models which had been successful, and so on. I suggested various possibilities for things he might start, but each was met with Ian's insistence that he wanted 'something different'.

Fieldnotes: 21 March

. . . I then said why not just look through the Resources Room and the Stock Cupboard to see if we could find some interesting materials that might give us an idea.

We inspected various types of card, off-cuts of wood, old shop display units and so on. I made various suggestions as to how they might be used. Ian wanted to know where all the bits and pieces had come from. We searched and examined in this way for some five minutes or so before Ian noticed a box containing packets of potato crisps and potato sticks. He said, almost at once, 'I know what I could do with them.' Assuming this to be one of Ian's little jokes and that he envisaged a quick snack, I replied, 'I bet!' But he was being quite serious. He explained that he could use them to make a collage. What an idea! Since the crisps and sticks were intended for use at some school function, I suggested Ian ask the headteacher before taking them as art materials. Ian soon gained this permission and returned to the classroom with one packet of each.

When Ian then said that he would do a ship with his crisps and sticks, I was somewhat disappointed assuming that he meant one of his battleships. How would he manage the straight lines with the sticks and crisps which are so irregular and easily shatter when cut? Nevertheless, Ian soon set to work.

I then realised that Ian was not making a modern battleship, like those of his previous drawings, but an oldfashioned sailing warship. For this the material seemed much more suitable. The outline of the ship — its hull, masts and gun holes — was made of relatively straight potato sticks. Projecting pieces were added to the bow and stern (as figure heads, I believe) and there was a lifeboat in tow. Ian had carefully selected two different shades of blue paper for the sea and sky onto which the sticks and crisps were stuck. For the horizon and the waves he added carefully chosen curved sticks. Billowing sails were made of the largest crisps he could find and others were used as clouds.

The finished result is most effective having taken no more than an hour to complete.

Throughout the work, Ian resisted any temptation to eat the crisps or sticks, as also did the several children who gathered around him. Apart from one or two comments of wastefulness, everyone took Ian's task seriously and many approved of the result.

The point at which Ian saw the link between his current interests and the possibilities offered by the materials is most striking. He was immediately able to see the crisps and sticks as having a function so very different from the accepted one. He quickly decided that his collage would be of a boat, without discussion of the matter; indeed one might say that he saw the materials as a potential boat. Perhaps he was attracted by the relatively straight lines of the potato sticks and the contrasting irregularities of the crisps as elements from which a picture might be constructed. While his decision on the surface appears somewhat eccentric, it clearly related to his present interests and so for him was not such an unnatural interpretation. From his work, it becomes clear that his ideas about how a boat may be represented develop in response to the limitations and possibilities of the new material. He sees that an 'old fashioned' ship is a more appropriate subject for such material and that, far from being constrained by the uneven lines of the sticks and crisps, he exploits these characteristics most effectively.

The significance for me of this type of activity — a child's search for a stimulus to which to respond — was not primarily the educational value of such a process, but that on such occasions the essentially active interpretational and intentional nature of perceiving a stimulus and responding to it was most apparent.

But this interpretational feature does not only apply to the initial selection and use of materials. Often, once a child had started to work with a material, one activity led naturally to another. Now the material may be seen as a trigger which sets off a sequence of events. Initially the material was used for a particular purpose. The resulting work itself was then interpreted, in response to which further development took place. Such was the case when David, playing with some very acute-angled wooden triangular blocks, put some together to make a ramp. He soon saw how he could use more blocks to extend the ramp backwards. Seeing this as a slipway for a lifeboat, he went on to make the lifeboat, its trailer and a winch by which it could be hauled up into its shed. Batteries and bulbs were then used to construct a lighting system and finally he wrote poems about lifeboats. David spent most of his time for a week struggling with the problems raised by each stage of the work. A sequence like this may be called 'open-ended' because its course could not have been foreseen by teacher or child at the outset. But the development was purposive and rational because at each stage David was able and permitted to make his own interpretation of the situation and to act according to it. It was in this that his control of the activity consisted.

Often in work which followed a sequence such as this, the child would see completed stages of the work in a different light, suggesting new objectives for the activity. In the process, ideas crystallized and intentions became more clearly defined. A process such as this is familiar to anyone who has tried to express and develop their ideas through writing. As Michael Armstrong once put it in a memo he wrote on my field notes: 'Often, in my own writing, there is an overall idea which, in the process of being written out, becomes transformed, perhaps by some chance discovery of an appropriate word that changes my conception, perhaps by revisions in my thought as I try to get from a vague idea in my mind to precise words on the page.'

While such a sequence is almost impossible to follow clearly in respect of a child's (or anyone else's) writing, I was often able to trace its development when working alongside a child who is using concrete materials. The first striking example of this occurred in the second week of the fieldwork as I observed Karen at work and talked to her about it.

Fieldnotes: 11 September
Karen had been at the group last Thursday when Chris Harris introduced the shapes and sticky paper. Using the shaped tiles as stencils, she had cut out of sticky paper a square, trapezium, rhombus and semicircles, and made these into a man. His shape was simple: a square (as diamond) for a body, circular head, trapezoidal hat tilted, narrow rhombus arms and legs and semi-circular feet. Using dark and light green paper, the result was most effective. This figure occupied the left third of the paper. Next to it, and in no apprent relation to the man at the time, she made a tessellating design using the narrow rhombi.... When she continued with her work this morning, she remarked to me that the tessellated design reminded her of an ear of corn. She then continued to work with this in mind. The central part of the ear she made up of two adjacent columns of tessellated rhombi, each rhombus appearing to correspond to an individual seed stacked one above the other and coloured alternatively pink and blue. To each side of the ear were set at an angle further lines of rhombi in light green and black. It became

clear that these lines represented the hairs or feathers which surround an ear of barley. (Last week, together with the rest of the class she had watched a field of barley being harvested. She later told me how she remembered the combine harvester and how the ears of barley looked.)

The completed ear was extremely effective, suggesting the close packing of the seeds, the spikiness of the hairs and the change of colour contrasting the two features. The whole was set at a slight angle to the vertical.

43

Karen then continued to 'play' with the rhombus tiles and soon found that she could make them into a twelve-pointed star by placing all the narrow angles together in the centre. So she cut out twelve rhombi, six from each of two slightly differing shades of red sticky paper.

While she was doing this I was also playing with the shapes beside her using the paper she had cut out. She saw me place two shapes like this, and said, 'That looks like a bird.' She then added that she was not going to make a star after all but would have birds flying around the ear of corn and the farmer. She quickly stuck down pairs of rhombi (one dark red, one light red) as the birds, each at a different angle. In spite of the speed with which she worked, the angle and positioning of each 'bird' was such as to provide balance to the picture.

She then told me, after some conversation with a friend with whom she was working, that they were not, after all, to be 'birds', but 'butterflies'. To make the change she stuck two narrow strips of red for antennae onto the upper angle formed by the two rhombi. The piece was now complete.

In Karen's work her changes in intention and interpretation and their relation to past experience are quite clear. The 'Man', originally suggested by the shapes considered discretely, later became 'The Farmer'. A tessellating experiment suggests an ear of corn, later identified as barley as she relates it to her observations of the harvesting. Another tessellating experiment leads to a star which is then rejected, for aesthetic reasons, after she takes up my shape which she sees as a bird. 'Birds' are then transformed into butterflies, small additions being required as if to confirm or ratify the change of perception.

The materials with which Karen was working were such as to impose few limitations on the final design. After the first day she chose to work only with the acute-angled rhombi, and her work with these may be seen as a kind of experimentation. But this was her choice. The material and wide variety of shapes available to her did not constrain her to working in this way. Comparing her initial construction of the man with the later stages of the work, where she was using only rhombi and aspects of formal design became paramount, it is clear that the focus of the work sharpened as it proceeded.

This feature of increasing refinement or focus of the objectives of the work was often apparent. It appeared that when the materials themselves were 'open-ended', through their successive interpretations, the children would impose a structure upon them and thus upon their activity. There was a contrasting development when the children were working with highly structured materials, for example, a piece of mathematical apparatus or work card designed to develop a particular concept or skill. Then they were constrained to work according to this structure, to utilize and understand it as best they could, rather than to create one for themselves. It appeared that the resulting activity's structure differed not so much in degree as in its origins.

But even the materials which were open to a wide range of uses often posed severe limitations upon how the children's work could progress. The vital factor now was how the children would respond to these constraints. Would they be frustrated in their desire to exercise a controlling influence over their work, or would they exploit these constraints to their advantage? In other words, how would the limitations imposed by the materials affect the children's ability to structure their activity?

Inspired, I think, by some pattern making activities that his friends David and Greg had become involved in, Ian announced to me one afternoon that he would make a pattern by counting along the squares on graph paper. The development of this activity sheds some light on these questions.

Fieldnotes: 16 October
When I returned to the group, this is what Ian had completed (see Diagram 1).

It was quite clear from watching him draw this, and by examining the completed pattern, that Ian had used no rule of construction. He had merely counted on as many squares as he wished before changing direction. (This is not to say that he may not have taken into account aesthetic considerations.) The pattern was not 'mathematical'. Note also, that pattern (1) finishes when Ian reaches the edge of the paper.

Intending to encourage Ian to use some kind of rule to construct his series, I suggested that instead of counting just any number of squares along for each line, he might first count 'one', then 'two', then 'three' and so on. Then, counting together, I wrote down the numbers from 1 to 13 for him to follow.

Ian took up this idea and soon completed his second

(1)

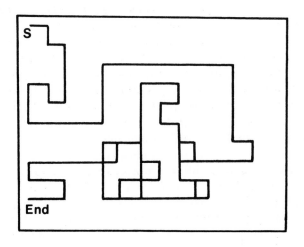

(2)

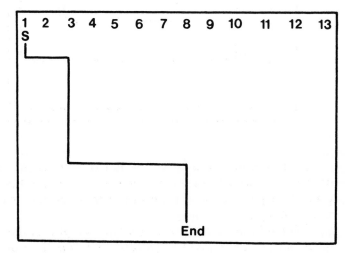

pattern (see Diagram 2). Again the end was determined by the edge of his paper. Note also that the second vertical should have been 3 and not 4: Ian has missed out 3.

When I pointed out this mistake, Ian was keen to start again (see Diagram 3). He wrote down the numbers up to 13 on a new sheet of graph paper (later adding 14 and 16 but missing out 15) and proceeded from the top left. This time, when he reached point A (correctly), he decided to change direction upwards to B instead of downwards. He explained later that this was because there was not room on the paper to count 7 squares down to B. Using similar reasoning, he was forced to turn left from B to C and left again from C to D and so on.

(3)

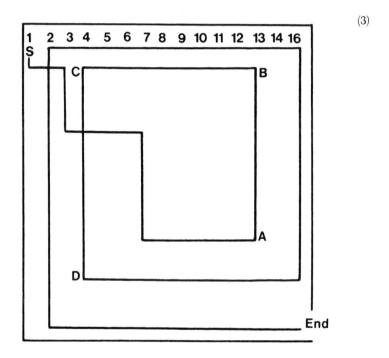

There are errors in his counting (AB is 8 instead of 7), but his pattern was beginning to take on a spiral rather than a stepped shape. Again, the pattern ends when Ian reaches the edge of his paper.

I did not discuss his work with him except to suggest that he might like to make another pattern, but this time on a much larger sheet of graph paper. While I did not mention this to Ian, I wondered what effect the larger sheet would have on his strategy. Would he take advantage of the possibility it offered of continuing with the steps or would he concentrate on the spiral, or would he again mix the two?

After lunch Ian took up my suggestion and I gave him a sheet of centimetre squared graph paper measuring 70 cm by 55 cm. Initially he copied his previous pattern (3) making steps up to 6 (point A). From there he started a clockwise spiral up to 13 (point B). He then turned left instead of right, thus breaking the spiral. He explained later that this was because, were he to continue this spiral, he would soon be led off the edge of the paper. From B he started another clockwise spiral, continuing to point C.

(4)

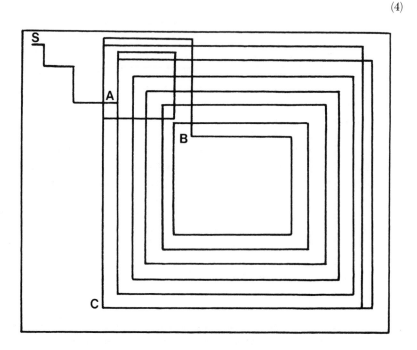

Two lines before C Ian said to me, 'I want to cut across the middle here', pointing to the unpatterned area in the centre of this second spiral. He then added, 'But I can't, because every step I go further outwards, the numbers are too big to take me back to the middle.' Then, when he reached C, he seemed suddenly to see the solution to his problem. He explained how if he made the numbers go down, 36, 35, 34, ..., he would then be able to work backwards towards the centre. So from C he counted upwards 35 (instead of 37 it would have been had he continued the spiral outwards). From here the last two or three stages are difficult to interpret, and he did make one or two errors in counting. He then stopped, saying that he would like to start again on the other side of the paper.

It was clear by now that Ian was committed to the spiral. Earlier in the afternoon I had asked him why he had started his drawing at the top left corner and why he had chosen to do the steps rather than start with the spiral. Having finished this pattern, he now said, 'So you see why I did the steps bit first. I had to get to the middle of the paper to do my spiral.' It did not occur to him to start spiralling in the middle, indeed he appeared to be following a rule that the pattern should start at the top left.

While Ian expressed his reasoning very clearly, it may have been a post hoc rationalization of what he had done. But nonetheless it showed that he now clearly grasped the nature of this kind of spiral.

Before Ian started on his next spiral I said that I thought there was no reason why he should not start in the middle of the page if he so wished. He was at first concerned as to how he would find the middle point. I suggested that it would be near enough if he guessed.

Ian then worked quickly on his own, making the new spiral. Twice I interrupted him to point out an error in his counting, but otherwise he worked confidently without mistakes. He soon saw how each successive layer of the spiral moved outwards by two squares. He also found that time could be saved by measuring with a cm ruler rather than by counting squares. He thus completed, without error, a square spiral up to '38'. Then, seeing the path between the lines as a track, he closed the spiral with a short arm from the final point to the adjacent line. He then said he would colour the track and make his spiral into a counting game. This he would work on tomorrow.

When Ian arrived at school the following day, he told me how he would not make a game out of his track as he had decided. Instead, he would make yet another spiral, this time even larger so that it filled the whole large sheet of the squared paper. He wanted to display this for the other children to see. But this time he was not content merely to guess the mid-point of the sheet of paper before starting. He wanted to find it exactly so that his spiral could be as large as possible. To do this, he did not consider folding the sheet but, using only a 30 cm ruler, developed an ingenious and thoroughly logical method for finding the centre point by a process of increasingly accurate approximations, which involved him in counting no higher than ten at a time. His procedure involved seven distinct operations which he was later able to explain to me most articulately. Having found the centre point he went on to construct a spiral filling the sheet without assistance from me. We then pinned it up on the wall and this sequence of work was finished.

Ian's work here bore no relation to that of David and Greg from whose ideas it originated. He worked mostly on his own, occasionally calling me over to view what he had done, while at times I would sit by him saying little.

My only major interventions, my suggestions that he use positive integers as a construction rule and later that he work on larger sheets of paper, no doubt had considerable influence on the course of the work, though he may well have come to these decisions on his own. But the major developments in Ian's plans stemmed from the way in which his material, the squared paper, impinged upon his work and the way in which he made use of its limitations. It was the boundaries of the paper which determined the 'end' of his early patterns, and later suggested to him that the pattern could be 'bent round'. His decision here led to the development of the spiral. This spiral then suggested a purpose to the activity — the making of a track game — but this was later dropped in favour of more spiral making. This led to his decision to find the mid-point of his paper accurately, which he did in a way appropriate to his level of mathematical skill.

While Ian's pattern making was not rigidly determined by the nature of the graph paper, in that it could have developed in countless other ways, his reaction to the material's limitations was such as to develop a more orderly and clearly defined purpose to his activity. Through a succession of developing interpretations and intentions, what was initially chaotic in method and vague in aim, becomes precise in method and clear in aim. It was Ian's readiness to reinterpret his work at each stage, encouraged by only the minimum of conversation with me, that enabled him to maintain control over it and avoid the kind of 'aimless activity' of which the HMIs complain. Once control was regained, the work could continue in an exploratory fashion, but with a new and increased sense of direction.

But it was not only the constraints imposed by the materials which were exploited by the children to their own advantage. Often accidents or their own mistakes would be given a new meaning and significance in a way which led them to reinterpret their activity.

Michael Armstrong, in a chapter on art and representation,[3] showed how a child's painting could be viewed as an interplay between accident and intention as the child interpreted unintended effects and then incorporated them into the unfolding purposes of the work. I was interested to see whether this concern to exploit the accidental would be a characteristic of more mathematical or scientific explorations, explorations which appeared to be governed by tighter rules. Clearly, making rules (whether in a playground game or mathematical investigation) is one way that children exercise control over their activity. How then do the children deal with the accident or mistake, which by its nature poses a threat to those rules, without losing their control over the activity?

Julie and Louise often made up games together. The way in which they accommodated an accidental encounter into a game they had invented proved to be a striking example, but one that was characteristic of the approach of many of the children in Chris Harris's class.

Fieldnotes: 4 December
... They said that they would make up a game of treasure hunt. They explained how the idea of this game was to set a series of instructions which would lead a hunter to the treasure.

They practised these ideas outside, but due to the cold, wet weather, they soon returned to continue indoors. They showed me one of their sets of written instructions: '10 up — 3 to the right — 1 back — turn around to face the other way — 5 up — 1 right — 2 up — 3 to left — 2 up — 5 right.'

They both showed me in the classroom how these instructions should be followed. Louise said, 'There isn't much room in the classroom so we'll have to use fairy steps instead of paces....' We talked about how we might continue the idea indoors. I suggested that squared paper could be used to draw the path to the treasure.... They went off on their own to make up sets of instructions. When I next saw Julie, she explained how she had made up a set which returned you to the starting place.

In the afternoon Julie and Louise went outside to try out these instructions. I accompanied them. The first two instructions, starting from an arbitrarily selected point, took them to the base of the climbing frame. (This is a cubic lattice of bars.) Louise read out her next instruction to Julie, who was being the 'hunter': '2 up'. (In the written instruction this, of course, meant '2 forward'.) Julie said, excitedly, 'Look! I can really go upwards', and proceeded to climb up two rungs of the climbing frame. However, following Louise's further written instructions would have led her up in the air over the top of the frame. Realizing this, Louise changed her instructions so that Julie could continue going up, down, right and left on the frame. Their 'treasure hunt' had now taken off into three dimensions. They now had to distinguish between 'up' and 'forwards', and between 'down' and 'backwards'.

I left them to continue on their own.

When I returned twenty minutes later they were working out a much more complex set of instructions. This involved climbing over a horizontal bar (separate from the frame), pacing to the frame, climbing up it and into the middle, hanging, dropping and crawling so as to return to the starting point. Julie slowly walked through the course while they discussed how to name each manoeuvre unambiguously and, in as few words as possible. Meanwhile, Louise wrote down what they decided to be the instructions. With the set complete, and Julie returned to the starting point, Louise then followed the same instructions. This also took her around the same course, finishing at the starting point, and thus served as something of a check to the instructions.

Here the repercussions of the accidental encounter with the climbing frame are quite dramatic. They could so easily have chosen to avoid it by starting the instruction following sequence again. They chose not to because they saw the relationship between the structure of the frame and the structure of the game they were playing. They were thus able to see the frame as being open to the same kind of exploration. However, since it presented a bounded three-dimensional partitioning of space rather than one which was un-bounded and two-dimensional, they realized that their instructions would have to be refined in order to avoid ambiguity (for example, to distinguish between 'up' and 'forward') and to account for the frame's boundaries (so as to avoid the hunter's having to climb higher than the top of the frame). They further realized that instructions guiding the hunter over and under bars would be more difficult to word precisely. It was of the essence of the original game that instructions should be written before the actual 'hunt' begins. But the difficulties of doing this led them to adopt their 'walking through' procedure as the instructions were being written. When Louise finally walked through the instructions which she had already written, it served as something of a check on them. These written instructions were a successful attempt to record a complex set of manoeuvres in as simple a way as possible.

Their encounter with the frame offered Julie and Louise a challenge to incorporate it into their strategy. What is clear from their response is their readiness to accept the challenge, their ability to interpret the frame in terms of this strategy, and the effect this had upon the mathematical and linguistic demands which the activity made upon them.

We can understand Julie's and Louise's incorporation of the climbing frame into their game as an attempt to make sense of the accidental encounter in terms of their prior plans and strategies, which were then adapted in order to accommodate it. But the accident itself was not actively sought.

However, in a process of enquiry, the type of activity I now want to consider, the situation is changed. No one approaches an enquiry without some prior hypotheses, priorities or ways of looking at things, and its purpose may indeed be to test or refine such ideas. But, in general, an enquiry is concerned to account for a range of phenomena, which may initially appear unrelated, or 'accidental', in order to discover their relationships. Whether as an archaeologist excavating the site of an ancient city, or as a child observing the swings of a pendulum the enquirer actively seeks those features and irregularities which require explanation.

It would seem, however, that the child's enquiry is somewhat different from the adult's. Adults are inclined to work within boundaries described by the different disciplines of thought. Children, on the other hand, appear to integrate these different disciplines largely

Key
<<<<Embankments
1   Old bridge
2   New bridge
3   Site of first lock gate
4   Site of second lock gate
5   Concrete dam
6   Old sluice gate and mill race
7   Weir

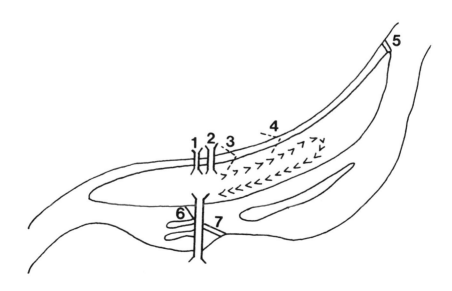

because they are unaware of the distinctions which adults perceive to exist between them.

The integrated nature of children's enquiries was very apparent when the class went on a series of visits to Hoby Field Study Centre. The area of study consisted of a river which parts around a large central island. On one side of this is a stream which more or less follows the course of a disused canal. On the other side of the island the river flows over a weir. The stream and river meet again further upstream.

On the first visit to the area the children made sketch maps, drawings and dipped for water creatures. They were told little, if anything, of the history of the area. It was this aspect which was to concern a group of six children with whom I spent the morning of the second day. We walked to the old bridge (1).

Fieldnotes: 19 September
... We then examined the canal retaining wall immediately upsteam from the bridge. The canal now had only a shallow steam flowing along its bed. It must have been deeper in the days when it was used by barges. Helen suggested that the water might not in fact have been higher in the canal, but that the canal might have just filled up with bits of masonry, rocks and silt. There were thus two possibilities: either (a) the water level used to be higher, or (b) the canal bed used to be deeper, (or some combination of (a) and (b)). We began to look for evidence to test these two possibilities. One of the children noticed that the bricks underneath the bridge were a darker green up to a point about $1\frac{1}{2}$ metres above the present water level. This suggested that the level had been higher.

Then Susan noticed two vertical curved indentations in the sides of the retaining wall. I suggested that these might have been the hinge recesses of a pair of lock gates which have since disappeared. Several of the children saw that if there had been a pair of lock gates here, then there must have been another pair further upsteam. There was then general excitement as the children charged off into the undergrowth, which now almost filled the canal bed, to look for evidence of another pair of gates.

Soon, shouts of 'we've found it' came from somewhere upstream. Sure enough, they had found identical markings in the wall remains some 20 metres upstream. . . .

We then noticed on the canal bed at this point a mass of heavy permanent planking. Someone suggested that this provided a seal at the bottom of the lock gates. This, together with the discoloration of the bricks under the bridge, convinced us that the water level had indeed fallen since the canal was in use.

We continued upsteam. There was no longer any evidence of the canal retaining wall. We then came to a more recently constructed small concrete dam at the point where the stream joined the main river. Robert said that this had been built in order to divert the flow of water away from the canal bed, but, since it had been holed, this accounted for the small stream which now flowed along the bed. . . .

The children inspected the old sluice gate and mill race. There was virtually no evidence of the old mill which we presumed to have been built there, except for the occasional piece of rubble in the bed of the river and a piece of stone and mortar jutting through the grass on the bank. . . .

Chris Harris then called the children together and pointed out the configuration of embankments which he and I had been discussing while apart from the children. He asked if they could think of any explanations.

Julie suggested that perhaps there had been another 'kind of river' between the canal and the main river and that these embankments were the remains of its banks. Someone else suggested that such a 'river' would act as a passing place so that barges could draw in here to let other barges coming in the opposite direction pass by. Helen said that she thought the barges would moor here while they were loaded and unloaded. Susan said, 'Yes, that's where they'd unload the coal.' Helen said that it was wheat that would be delivered to the mill; Julie, that flour would be collected from the mill. The conversation became quite excited at this point as the children pictured the scene as it may have been many years ago.

We then examined the sluice gate and remaining piece of wall retaining the mill race. We found no evidence of where a mill wheel might have been secured, but the children soon clambered down onto the rocky river bed and found several pieces of masonry which they assumed to have fallen from the old mill. They also spotted a piece of old timber jutting up from the river bed. It was suggested that this was the remains of an earlier bridge and the children searched for more evidence of such a bridge, but none was found.

Finally, we returned to the old bridge and the site of the first pair of lock gates. Helen explained how further markings she had observed above the hinge recesses corresponded to the angle at which the gates would have closed. . . .

Many questions had been raised, and perhaps many of our hypotheses had been wrong, but everyone had been involved in searching for evidence, making sense of it, and building up a picture. . . .

When we returned to the study area the following day, Julie said that she wanted to make drawings of how the area might have looked a hundred years ago. Between sketching, she walked with me from the old bridge up the canal bed, explaining things as she went. She spoke fluently and needed no prompting or leading questions from me.

Fieldnotes: 21 September
... She described to me how the boats would come up the canal as far as the first lock gate, then wait for it to open and pass through. When it closed behind them, and the water level had risen between the sets of gates, men would carry the sacks of grain from boats up to the door which was behind the grain store. She said that there must have been a bakery nearby which would have made bread from the flour. She asked if the canal went through Hoby village. I said that I thought that unlikely since the village was up on a hill. She then said that either they would have carted the sacks of flour up to the village, or else the bakery must have been near the site of the mill.

As we approached the supposed site of the second pair of lock gates, Julie continued her explanation of how locks enabled a boat to go uphill. The only aspect that puzzled her was how a sluice gate operates to allow water to by-pass closed lock gates....

The striking feature of these enquiries is the children's readiness to account for every little irregularity. Each becomes the basis for some hypothesis to be later refined or discarded in the light of new evidence. At one moment they focus upon the mechanical problems of how a lock works, at the next upon aspects of social history connected with the siting of a bakery. But these diverse aspects are integrated as they build up an overall picture.

It is also of interest that the children rarely made requests for specific knowledge from me or the other teachers involved. No doubt they realized that I in fact had little knowledge of the history of the area. But when I suggested, at one point, that we could perhaps find out more about it from the books at the Study Centre, or that I might be able to find some more knowledgeable adult to ask, they were unenthusiastic. It seemed that they were involved in a kind of imaginative game which, while it had to take account of a wide range of observed phenomena, was concerned primarily with constructing a coherent and complete picture, rather than the search for some objective truth. Imagination and reality were finely interwoven and to have 'found out the answer' from an external source would, no doubt, have denied them the essential imaginative element of the activity. Their approach is somewhat like that of the archeologist trying to discover new facts at the very frontiers of existing knowledge, for now there *is* no final authority that can be appealed to; hypotheses must be constructed upon the basis of new evidence.

The pictures the children built up in this way were bold in their completeness. The details Julie gave of where the flour would have been taken, the positioning of the bakery, her theory concerning the embankments and so on present a picture which is complete and yet, for this very reason, is highly improbable. As a theory, it explains a wide range of data, but yet could easily be falsified by the emergence of new evidence. But this, according to a Popperian view of science, does not make it a 'bad theory'. On the contrary, 'the aim of the scientist is not to discover absolute certainty, but to discover better and better theories (or to invent more and more powerful searchlights) capable of being put to more and more severe tests (and thereby leading us to, and illuminating for us, ever new experiences). But this means that these theories must be falsifiable; it is through their falsification that science progresses.'[4] Of course, from an adult perspective, Julie's 'theory' had not been put to a severe test. But, granted the limitations in her experience, her knowledge and the evidence available to her, the approach appears to be similar to that of the Popperian scientist.

The characteristics of completeness, coherence and relative lack of interest in authoritative 'answers' were evident in much of the children's general enquiries. To a large extent this seemed to explain the relative lack of interest in books during the early stages of their investigations. For example, towards the end of the year many children spent at least a fortnight studying caterpillars and other insects, for which many useful reference books were provided. But these were little used during the first week. Dean, in his investigations into the taxonomy of caterpillars (see Chapter 2) had no intention of using books to tell him of the different species and their characteristics. It was only after he had developed and examined his own system for inventing names and sorting his caterpillars that he realized its limitations and hence the need for some objective system of classification. From then on, he frequently used a reference book. The book had become transformed from a catalogue of unrelated pictures, descriptions and facts, into a source of coherent information which he could use for his own purposes. Its authority was no longer remote and he could understand, in principle, how its information might have been gathered. He could thus control his use of the book.

This is not to suggest that books should be limited to the later stages of enquiry. Different books will be appropriate at different stages. The point is that, since the children were concerned to construct 'pictures' or 'systems' through their enquiries, books which present a ready packaged system were liable to pre-empt this process if used too early. For these 9- to 11-year-old children reference books represented a final authority on facts and the ways of finding them. It was only when they were able to reconstruct such knowledge in the light of their own experience that these books could help them in the construction of their systems.

This discussion of the children's enquiries has considerable implications for the general question of their control over their activity. For while their enquiries were directed toward the construction of systems which explained their own observations, rather than toward the discovery of established objective theories, there was no question of their becoming lost in the attempt to follow externally applied procedures or to understand theories for which they had insufficient background experience. They did of course meet established theories and procedures and were confronted with the second-hand experience of others through books, adults, the media and so forth. To suppose that they should not would support the totally unrealistic assumption that children can reconstruct a sufficient portion of human knowledge from their own direct experience. But while they had control over their enquiries, the points at which they confronted external ideas were largely under their control, as were the interpretations they made of them.

Throughout these last two chapters I have illustrated how, for the children with whom I worked, it was their ability to control their activity which was crucial for them to develop a structure to their work and a sense — albeit open to reinterpretation — of its purpose. What I want to go on to consider is how, within this framework of control, the quality of the children's thinking was revealed. For it became increasingly clear that this sense of control was not only an important factor in their learning, but provided a vital key for me, as teacher, to understand how it was they learnt.

Notes

1 Report of HMI (1978) *Primary Education in England*, Para. 3, p. 19.
2 *Ibid.*, Para. 3, p. 21.
3 ARMSTRONG, M., *op. cit.*, p. 55.
4 POPPER, K. (1972) *Objective Knowledge: An Evolutionary Approach*, p. 361.

Chapter 4

Abstract Thinking and Hypothesizing

In Chris Harris's classroom there were many opportunities for informal conversation. The children where relatively free to discuss their interests or personal concerns even where these did not directly relate to the actual tasks in hand.

In respect of such classroom talk I soon found myself in a somewhat privileged position in the class. Without the overall responsibility for running the class, the children soon realized that I could easily be drawn into their informal discussions. While at first I saw this primarily as an opportunity for getting to know the children and establishing a relationship of confidence between us, I later became more aware of the value of such talk for gaining insight into their individual concerns, their ways of conducting discussion and argument and the thinking which they applied to serious matters not directly related to their school work. We often talked in a casual manner about what they had done after school the previous day, or where they went for their summer holidays. But increasingly, I found myself drawn into more intense discussions ranging over such subjects as life-styles, sex-roles, religion, racial discrimination, jobs and politics (there was a general election during the summer term). It seemed that many of the older children, who would soon be transferring to their secondary schools, were becoming increasingly conscious of 'adult' and 'controversial' issues. No doubt some of the children were beginning, for the first time, to be aware of the extent to which adults disagree about important matters, that beliefs were subject to change and that the answers to their own questions were not always straightforward matters of fact to which an all-knowing teacher or parent has privileged access.

In this kind of discussion, the children would often appear to be grappling at the very frontiers of their knowledge and reasoning ability. Large areas of subject matter would begin to gain a significance at an emotional level often left untouched by more academic school work. In my own teaching I have found this to be one of the most rewarding aspects of working with the oldest children in the primary school. But what interested me now was the way in which children are able to organize their thinking in such spontaneous discussions, how they take account of differing views expressed by their friends and what this can show us of their ability to reason in what is often called an 'abstract' manner.

I remember David asking me, on several occasions, if I believed in God. He would often pose such difficult questions to me over lunchtime. I suspect he enjoyed the opportunity to rehearse, before a sympathetic audience, some clever argument he had got together. But there was also a genuine sense of enquiry on his part. He claimed he was a non-believer, arguing that if God made the world then something must have made God. But nothing could have made God, because such a thing would have had to exist before God which is impossible since God is supposed to have been the first 'thing'. Thus David's commitment to the belief that everything must be caused by something before it led him to maintain that God is impossible. The further arguments which arose during the course of the following discussion were not ones which we had previously talked about together.

Before this discussion started, I had no idea that we would end up talking about God. Initially, David was simply 'fishing around' for ideas.

Fieldnotes: 13 November

David approached me saying that he wanted to do something interesting with me, but did not know what. He then asked me what I studied at college. I said, 'Philosophy'. He said, 'What's that?' I made a vague reply saying that it was difficult to explain but that it concerned truth. Thinking further about what we might do, I suggested that it is often a good idea if you start your work with a question. Did he have any questions which concerned him? David sat thoughtfully for a moment and then said, 'Do you believe in God?' I replied, rather evasively, that I was not sure what God was. David went on to explain his reason for not believing in God because it was impossible to answer the question 'Who made God?' After briefly discussing this point I suggested that it might be more interesting if David were to continue the argument with someone who was a convinced Christian.

So David got up and found Helen and Julie who had said they were Christians. They enthusiastically agreed to join in a discussion about God and left their writing to join us.

During the discussion that followed, I kept running notes on what was said recording most of it verbatim. These notes provided some structure to the discussion and were referred to at times where clarity was needed. They thus served purposes of the children as well as my own enquiry. Throughout, I acted as a neutral chairman and did not introduce new ideas into the discussion. Afterwards, we went through my notes together to check that I had got it right and to provide them with the opportunity of reviewing their arguments.

Discussion on God

1.   (David opened by asking Helen and Julie if they were Christians.)
Julie: Yes.
Helen: Yes.

5.   *David*: Do you believe in God?
Julie, Helen: Yes.
David: Why?
Julie, Helen: Because we're Christians.
David: Why are you Christians?

10.   *Julie*: Because of the legends in the Bible.
Helen: Who else could have made all things? God is a symbol is kindness.
Julie: He's a spirit.
David: But why, then, doesn't God make me believe in

15.   Him?
Julie: He's not really got control.
(On re-reading the notes, Julie said that she had really meant: 'He doesn't want everyone to believe in Him.')
Helen: He likes you to do as you please. It's a free world.

20.   *David*: Why does God let wars happen?
Julie: There wouldn't be a President of the United States if it wasn't for wars. We don't know everything. These wars could be good, or they could be bad, we don't know.

25.   *Helen*: We have wars becuase different countries believe in their own rights.
David: But thousands get killed for no reason.
(Julie and Helen replied that people go to war for their Queen or their country.)

30.   *David*: Why have battles? Why doesn't God do it? (He explained that he meant 'why doesn't God solve the problems which lead to war?')
(Julie and Helen both reiterated their point that God does not wish to control the world.)

35.   *Helen*: People (fight to) defend their laws.
Julie: Some people want to satisfy their Queen and so on.

(There then followed further unrecorded discussion of this point, but no substantially new argument.)

David: Who made God?

40.   *Helen*: God is a miracle.

Julie: God made Jesus and Jesus did most of the work.

David: But who made the miracle?

Helen: *Nobody* makes a miracle. Miracles just *are*. God *is* a miracle.

45.   (Further unrecorded discussion.)

Helen: We believe through our families; father to father and so on.

(Next, my only significant intervention. At my suggestion Helen and Julie asked David why did he not believe in 50.   God.)

David: If God exists, who made God? If God is a spirit who made the spirit?

Helen: No, but God is a miracle. Nobody *makes* miracles.

(She explained that she had already made this clear.)

55.   *David*: Who made Adam and Eve?

Julie: We don't know. We believe what we're told; what's in the Bible.

(They then added that they did not believe everything anyone tells them but that they do, for example, believe 60.   their teacher.)

(David then suggested that they look in the Bible to see what it says. Together they examined the first verses of Genesis 1 which Helen read aloud.)

David: That's not what the scientists say.

65.   (Helen said that since scientists know more than other people about science they are in a position to deceive the rest of us.)

(However, she then explained that the world was made 'like a big volcano'. The cracks in the world then filled up 70.   to become rivers, the larger ones forming lakes and seas. The moon was a bit that was blown off.

She said this was what she believed but that other people might believe differently, we didn't really know. Julie agreed with this account. They both said that God made 75.   the world before this explosion. David then interrupted. . . .)

David: Excuse me! What did he make the world out of?

Helen: Clay.

Julie: No, don't be silly. There wouldn't have been any clay 80.   before the earth was made.

Helen: Oh yes. It wasn't clay. It was a miracle.

(David then returned to the question of war, in particular World War II.)

85.   *Helen*: We think that the Germans started it. They think we started it. God says that they should do what they think is right.

(The discussion then returned to the source of belief. Helen and Julie said that people believed what their parents believed. They then argued about whether or not

90.   this was a Christian school. Julie and Helen said it was.)

   David: No it's not. I'll do a survey.

   Helen: I bet you'll be outvoted. It's just that your family doesn't believe in God. They don't believe because their parents didn't believe.

95.   *David*: Yes, my Nan *does* believe in God. I'm challenging you to a survey!

   Helen: It'll cause trouble.

After a little more discussion, going over ground already covered, Julie and Helen returned to their table. Julie said she thought all this discussion was pointless, although her beliefs were important to her. Helen disagreed. She felt that we should discuss whatever is important to us. Helen appeared then to succeed in persuading Julie of this point. But Julie still maintained that one should stick to what one believes. 'It's like this project', Julie said, pointing to her folder of work. 'Once I've started it, I should stick to it until it's finished.' Helen said that belief in God is more important than a project and that one should therefore be prepared to be influenced by argument.

We then read over my notes and Julie made the slight, but important change (lines 17–18). They verified my account of what had been said.

There was then some discussion among all of us as to how a survey might be conducted without causing offence or embarrassment to anyone. This was not completed by the end of the day and further discussion in the classroom was provoked by the survey.

This discussion bears analysis in some detail. But first, to summarize the main strands of argument:

1 *Lines 14–19*. David argues that if God were omnipotent, He would make him believe. Helen and Julie reply that He wants men to be free to believe as they wish. The change Julie made, on reading my notes, from 'He's not really got control' to 'He doesn't want everyone to believe Him' is most important since it demonstrates that she recognizes her initial point to be inconsistent with an omnipo-

tent God. As now expressed, the inconsistency is removed: God is omnipotent but grants man his freedom of belief. This point is made again in Lines 33–34 and Lines 85–86. This leads naturally to the second strand of argument, the problem of theodicy.

2   *Lines 20–24*. David implies that if there were a God, He wouldn't let wars happen. Julie's reply shows considerable insight. Since the existence of the President of the USA (assumed to be a good thing) required wars to happen, then wars, though they appear to be bad, may actually lead to a greater good, though we might not be aware of this because of our limited knowledge.

Julie's argument concerning freedom and theodicy here is somewhat similar to the argument of Leibniz that God created the best of all possible worlds. Here is Russell's summary of Leibniz's argument:

> Free will is a great good, but it is logically impossible for God to bestow free will and at the same time decree that their should be no sin. God therefore decided to make men free, although he foresaw that Adam would eat the apple, and although sin inevitably brought punishment. The world that resulted, although it contains evil, has a greater surplus of good over evil than any other possible world; it is therefore the best of all worlds, and the evil that it contains affords no argument against the goodness of God.[1]

3   *Lines 39–44*. Here David hints at the argument he has often presented to me. Helen's response takes him somewhat by surprise as it is not one that David or I had previously considered together. Helen conceives of a miracle as not requiring a cause and thus God was not created. She repeats her point in Lines 53–54. On discussing this point later with me, she explained how most things happen 'for a reason', but that miracles are an exception to this rule. The strength of David's argument rests upon his assumption that everything has a cause. Now this assumption is challenged, he is unable to pursue his point directly, but later appeals to 'what the scientists say' (Line 64).

4   *Lines 56–60*. Julie now pursues the argument from a different angle concerning the cause of belief rather than its justification. This aspect is taken up again in the final part of the discussion (from Line 87). Julie and Helen accept the authority of the Bible and their parents. But David disputes that everyone accepts the belief of their parents since (Line 95) one of his parents chose not to accept the belief of their mother (that is, David's 'Nan'). Therefore, the fact that one's parents believe in God is not a sufficient reason for believing oneself.

While during the discussion there was considerable repetition of the various points, the flow of the argument was considerably logical and coherent. David has in mind the arguments he wishes to present and is quick to spot the opportunities afforded for him to make them. He plays the major role in structuring the discussion. Nevertheless, Julie and Helen, in replying to his 'cross-examination', see the need for consistency as well as plausibility. Julie's amendment on reading the notes concerning God's control over man (Lines 17–18) and her correction of Helen concerning the creation of the world (Lines 79–80) demonstrate her awareness of the need for consistency.

The final point concerning the origins of their faith and parental authority, they immediately see as relating to the practical question of whether or not the children in the school are in fact Christians. David's 'challenge' to a survey here is altogether appropriate.

This discussion was preceded by David asking me what philosophy is. While I was unable to reply satisfactorily, feeling that any such attempted explanation would be beyond his comprehension, it is now clear that these children have some ability to investigate some of its problems.

Of course, the beliefs which Helen, Julie and David express here are likely to have been influenced and to a large extent determined by those of their parents, friends and relations and the broader society in which they live. The arguments they produce in support of these are unlikely to have been purely of their own invention. But nevertheless, from the form of the discussion it is clear that their ideas were not blindly accepted. While Julie and Helen are only too ready to admit that their beliefs resulted from what they knew of the Bible and what their parents had told them, the manner in which they represented such ideas in argument suggests that they were not merely voicing a doctrine upon which they had been brought up, but had reflected upon these ideas and reinterpreted them. Many of the ideas put forward and the flow of the argument itself suggest considerable reflective awareness. To be able to present in argument such propositions as: That if God existed he would make me believe in Him and since he doesn't therefore he doesn't exist (David); That it is the limitation of human knowledge that makes some good things appear bad (Julie); That scientists are in a position to deceive the rest of us (Helen) — suggests more than merely an acquaintance with certain sophisticated ideas. Rather, it presupposes an ability to focus the mind upon ideas remote and highly abstracted from immediate experience. Indeed, their ability to use such propositions critically, with due regard for such logical axioms as consistency and inter-relatedness, requires an awareness not only of the subject of their argument, but also of the manner in which it is to be expressed, that is, an awareness of the form of the argument itself. This exercise of critical faculties as demonstrated in their discussion suggests that their beliefs, while being socially derived, are a reconstruction of the ideas which have been communicated to them rather than a copy of such ideas.

Furthermore, the form of the argument between David and Julie and Helen strongly suggests that they have built up some kind of system to support their beliefs. They each express not an unrelated set of opinions, but an interrelated set of arguments and beliefs within a consistent framework. When Piaget speaks of the inability of children, below the age of about 12, to construct 'systems', he bases his theory largely upon the results of experiments designed to provide evidence for the existence of specific logical systems underlying the child's thinking. Of children less than about 12, he says:

> The child does not build systems. Those which he possesses are unconscious or preconscious in the sense that they are unformulable or unformulated so that only an external observer can understand them, while he himself never 'reflects' upon them.[2]

The evidence of the above discussion would appear to conflict with this claim. Piaget does not intend his age limits for the various stages of development to be rigidly invariable. However this, and many other examples of the work of the children in Chris Harris's class, indicates an ability to think in a way more characteristic of Piaget's formal operational period (claimed to start at around 12 years old) than of the concrete operational period (from 7 to 11).

Piaget's findings have been criticized[3] on the basis that the children's interpretations of the experimental situation often did not correspond to the intentions of the experimenter. They were often placed in unfamiliar situations which they interpreted in ways which conflicted with the assumed interpretations on which the tests were based. According to research which Donaldson quotes concerning earlier developmental stages, the child's performance improves when tests are constructed in a linguistic and cultural setting that is less abstract (in the psychological sense of being less remote from their everyday experience) and is therefore more meaningful to them.

However, any experimental setting is bound to cause problems concerning the meaningfulness of the test to the child. But when selected spontaneous activity, such as the above discussion, is analyzed, we can observe children grappling with ideas which are not only significant and meaningful to them, but which lead them to the frontiers of their reasoning ability. Because the children controlled the situation, they had the opportunity to use their language for their own purposes, were not compelled to interpret those of an experimenter, and were thus likely to operate at their highest level, a level at which they would be unlikely to work within the confines of an experiment.

No doubt Susan Isaacs had this in mind when she viewed Piaget's earlier work. Gardner says of her:

> I think it may be said that even in Piaget's earliest studies she would agree that what he claimed to be true of the thinking of young children did apply in many situations, for example, where questions were asked of children or thinking was required of them *by others*, but that their intellectual powers were sometimes released at a higher level, especially in situations of spontaneous investigations through their play.... Piaget had shown teachers the most that can be expected of young children in test situations or when receiving formal teaching.[4]

Writing, however, presents children with a very different set of problems from talking, as far as the organization of their thinking is concerned. Michael Armstrong had observed that the children he studied 'did not regard these problems simply as so many barriers to significant expression; rather they made use of the problems, expressively, as devices for liberating and controlling the imagination.'[5] It would seem that control of the imagination is an important prerequisite for abstract or philosophical thinking. Not surprisingly, therefore, it was the children's writing which often presented the clearest evidence of their ability to think in an abstract manner.

Some two months after the discussion between David, Helen and Julie, Karen's mind began to run on somewhat similar lines as she sat down to write. She was not concerned to express her ideas about God in a logical form. Her mode is altogether poetic, but nevertheless, underlying her writing is an ability to abstract, to place herself apart from actual experience, or, to use Margaret Donaldson's term, to 'disembed' herself from it. While the 'system' which her poem suggests is not supported by propositional argument, it nonetheless expresses an order and relatedness, a kind of mystical sense which can be made of the world.

Fieldnotes: 10 January
With the intention of encouraging the children to become more involved in writing, Chris Harris held a 'writing group' for about half the class this morning. At this group they discussed a short talk he had given earlier in the morning at a school meeting (assembly). At this meeting he had played the first part of Richard Strauss' 'Thus Spake Zarathustra' and had then read the opening verses of Genesis together with an explanation. He had emphasized that this account used to be believed by many people, but that now many did not know what to believe. That

was a question, he suggested, that the children might often consider as they grow older.

At the end of the morning Karen returned from the 'writing group' to show me her poem which she was obviously pleased with. . . .

Earth (a poem)
A planet is silent and still as still as
Can be.   No light,   NO darkness,
What planet could it be?
No trees.   NO beauty,
Its Just?   Just
What it is.   lonely no one to know.
No pet to cuddle
No sisters or brothers to play
No mums or dads to love its Just? what
it is
But   Then
There was a day
and there was night there was
love and sight beauty
Animals flowers trees clear blue waters
and golden sands and then there was
Me
born on Earth.

The devices Karen uses show not only an exceptional degree of literary skill and sophistication, but also considerable insight into the issue of which she writes.

She describes the world of the opening verse of Genesis, a world 'without form and void'. Contrary to the biblical version, she conceives such a world as not even having darkness. It is a thing without attributes: a subject without a predicate. The lines 'Lonely no one to know / No pets to cuddle / No sisters or brothers to play / No mums or dads to love' increase the effect of negation by being written without a subject. When she read the poem to me, she shrugged her shoulders at the question mark ('It's just?') indicating that not only could she not describe such a world, but that it was indescribable. (Karen's conception here of a world without any attributes is highly abstract and similar to Helen's idea, in the earlier discussions of God, of a miracle, as being an event without a cause. They are both aware of the impossible nature of such things in the normal world, but speculate that normal rules have to be broken in order to explain the Creation.)

The second part of the poem, effectively opened by 'But Then' (note the capital T) on a line of its own, sums up the story of creation whose final act (or purpose) was 'Me' signifying, probably, mankind, 'born on Earth'. Now we can name the planet since it has attributes and thus real existence.

But Karen has done more than write a poem of the story of creation. She reinterpreted it, excluded any reference to a purposeful God (essential to the Bible's story) and yet retained the significance of the story. Indeed her enigmatic rendering increases the mystery of it. The story has become one which is both secular and yet mystical.

Karen has used many devices skilfully: the way the lines have been arranged to enhance the meaning; the use of the question mark to signify the unknown and unknowable; capital letters ('NO darkness', etc.). She effectively places together concrete and abstract nouns: 'NO trees. No beauty.' Her use of the indefinite article for the first day: 'There was *a* day / and there was night' and the way she has used or omitted 'and' in the last few lines, are instances of her highly deliberate use of poetic techniques. . . .

Karen's emotional involvement in the subject matter of her poem is apparent. While this emotional response is controlled and reflective (as opposed to being passionate) it is nonetheless intense. Often, the children's greatest achievements in their work were accompanied by such intense, but controlled, emotion. Such involvement in no way prevented them from 'disembedding' themselves from the immediacy of their experience, or from reflecting upon it in an objective manner. On the contrary, their emotional involvement was evidence of the meaningfulness and significance of the subject matter to them and was thus a precondition of the highest exercise of their intellectual faculties.

In general, it appeared to be the reality or meaningfulness to the children of the object of their reflection (as evidenced not only by their emotional involvement but also by their control of the activity in which they confronted it) that determined the 'level' at which they operated, rather than the object's concreteness (as in a practical activity) or its abstraction (as in an argument about God).

It is often assumed that, when children are working practically with materials, they think in a way that is qualitatively different from when they are dealing with written language or other symbols. Work on a practical activity may often be successfully accomplished without recourse to the type of reflective thought which requires one to stand back from one's experience, or to 'disembed' one's thought. But nevertheless most practical tasks present problems of one kind or another. The solution of problems often requires one to weigh up alternatives, to make hypotheses or to investigate by some trial and error method. Such activity may involve a degree of reflection and deliberation similar to that which accompanies the effective use of symbols. Too rigid a distinction is often made between 'practical' work and 'practical' thinking on one hand and 'academic' work and 'intellectual' thinking on the other, as if the hands and the head were unrelated and autonomous organs of the body.

When the children controlled their practical activities, the degree of their emotional commitment to their work, and of the work's significance, appeared to be greater than when they were circumscribed by the prescriptions of work cards, textbooks and so on. The relationship between significance or meaningfulness and control here is very close. Activities where the children were in control (in the sense described in the previous two chapters) were ones in which they had provided or at least fully internalized (by active interpretations) the purposes of them. Where this was the case, inasmuch as their thinking was at an abstract level, it was the result of *their* abstraction. Ideas which were abstracted (for example, generalized propositions or hypotheses) seemed more likely to be understood and manipulated when the children themselves made the abstraction in the service of some goal of theirs than when the abstraction was made externally (for example, by a textbook) and then offered, ready-made, to them. With regard to the abstracting of concepts, it is no doubt this perception that underlies the observation of Vygotsky that 'practical experience shows that direct teaching of concepts is impossible and fruitless.'[6]

While Ian found many difficulties in his work with written language or mathematical symbols, he became intensely involved with model making. Observing him making a model aeroplane, it soon became clear to me that his difficulties in more accademic work could not be the result of any inability to think in an 'abstract' way. As a first stage in its construction, Ian had just cut a balsa wood strip which was to be the wing of his aeroplane. He wanted to find the exact mid-point of this wing from which he would secure the fuselage. His method was to count, one centimetre at a time, from each end of the wing. The point at which his countings merged was the mid-point. He had just made one such estimate of the mid-point.

Fieldnotes: 3 October
Then he turned the wing upside down, saying that he would now do it again as a check. He repeated the same procedure. When he compared his second solution to his first, he found that they were about a centimetre apart. Dissatisfied with this, he said he would now have to do it all over again since he could not choose, by inspection, which of the points was preferable.

He turned the wing over to its original face and, measuring along the opposite edge to his first measurement, repeated the counting to obtain a third 'mid-point'. On inspecting his result, he was pleased to find that his second and third solutions were directly opposite one another, when the wing was viewed edge on.

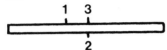

Numbers refer to order of measurement.
Wing viewed edge-on.

Ian was willing to accept the position (2/3) as the mid-point. But I suggested that he make just one more measurement on the same face of the wing as (2). He appeared happy to do this, and soon produced yet another mid-point at (4).

Middle section of wing enlarged. Viewed edge-on.

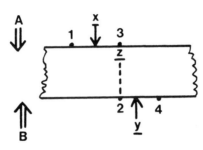

Naturally Ian was at first somewhat annoyed by this result, but his way of coping with the results was most interesting.

First he turned the wing over so that he viewed it from A (so that (2) and (4) were hidden). He then pointed to a position (x) (about mid-way between (1) and (3)) saying that it was probably the mid-point.

Then he turned the wing over and viewed it from B (so that (1) and (3) were now hidden). He now said that y (about midway between (2) and (4)) was probably the mid-point.

Finally, he viewed the wing edge on so that he could see all four solutions. He then said, with much more conviction, that z (that is, the 2/3 position) was the best place for the mid-point.

This was his final decision from which his modelling continued. . . .

In this work, my suggestion that Ian should make a fourth measurement had considerable implications for the thinking which he brought to bear on the task. His initial acceptance of the point 2/3 suggests that he conceives of the mid-point as being a point that can be conclusively discovered by measurement, and that his third

measurement confirmed the correctness of his second. This acceptance suggests that his thinking was something like: 'Either (1) was
correct or (2) was correct or both were wrong. But now since (3) is the
same as (2), then (2/3) must be correct and (1) incorrect.' Such a
conclusion on Ian's part is no doubt reasonable enough, but it
suggests that he takes a somewhat naive view of the nature of
measurement. More sophisticated reasoning leads us to conclude that
any such measurement as Ian made can only provide an approximation to the mid-point — a hypothesis as it were — and that in order to
make a more accurate approximation, or a more refined hypothesis,
successive measurements must be manipulated in some way (by, for
example, finding an average position). But such reasoning requires us
to disembed ourselves from the actual experience of measuring. We
have to operate not only upon the thing itself (by measuring it) but
upon the measurements we make of it. It also presupposes that we
conceive of a mid-point as being imaginary and hypothetical, rather
than actual and ascertainable, and therefore one step removed or
abstracted from direct experience. Such reasoning is often considered
to be inappropriate where children are involved in practical work
where only rough approximations are required.

But, for an aeroplane to fly on a level trajectory, the mid-point of
the wing must be established with some degree of accuracy. Ian was
aware of this since he decided to make a second measurement in spite
of the first measurement appearing to look right. He was prepared to
accept my suggestion to make a fourth measurement on the same
grounds. (Ian is normally only too ready to reject suggestions as to
how he should proceed.)

The way Ian deals with this fourth measurement demonstrates
that he is able to use the more sophisticated reasoning outlined above.
For in first saying that x was the mid-point (between (1) and (3) when
(2) and (4) were hidden) and then y (when (1) (3) and x were hidden),
he clearly recognized that mid-points are not discovered by any
particular measurement, but are more closely approximated by
operating upon such measurements. In judging x and then y to be the
mid-points he no longer conceives of one measurement as being
either right or wrong, but as being useful information from which he
might make some kind of average. Then, when he views the wing
edge-on and sees that x and y are different positions, he uses the same
reasoning to conclude that z — mid-way between x and y — is a
better result than either x or y. That z coincides with (2/3) no doubt
confirms his acceptance of this position. However, it is crucial here
that z is chosen not simply because it is the point which is corrobo-
rated by the second and third measurements, but because it is the
result of all four points being considered. While Ian's initial reaction
to the fourth reading was one of dismay, once he had interpreted its

significance by following the reasoning outlined here, it reinforced his commitment to *z* (or 2/3). Had Ian merely been following the more naive reasoning that he had appeared to in his earlier considerations of the first three measurements, then the fourth reading would have undermined, rather than reinforced his commitment to *z* since it would have required him to reject (4) as well as (1) as being incorrect. No doubt Ian may have said, had I asked him at the end of this work, that (1) and (4) were 'wrong' and (2) and (3) 'right'. But this would not conflict with the evidence that Ian had used all four measurements in arriving at his conclusion. It is the fact that he operated upon all four measurements rather than rejected the ones which did not corroborate the (2/3) position that demonstrates that he was working at a higher level of abstraction than is often recognized as being associated with practical activity.

In the examples of work so far, significance and meaningfulness for the children of what they were doing contributed to their ability to work at a higher level of abstraction. The same appeared to be the case in the activities where they invented rules to govern their work as, for example, in pattern making. When the rules were invented by the children (although perhaps with some guidelines, introduction or 'meta' rules suggested by the teacher) then they often showed considerable ability to reflect upon these rules.

Following their work on the Fibonacci series (see p. 31) David and Greg had used these and other repeating series of numbers to construct patterns on paper according to the following rule: 'Draw a line a number of units long which corresponds to the first term of the series; turn right; continue the line a length which corresponds to the second term; turn right; repeat for third term, etc. When all the terms have been exhausted continue the line using the first term again, and so on.' When Ian joined in this work later, he discovered,· to my initial surprise, that, however unrelated the numbers in the finite series might be, a very pleasing and regular pattern would emerge. Some weeks later, after Julie and Louise had invented their 'Treasure Hunt' game (see p. 51) I thought they might be interested to explore these kinds of patterns since they bore some similarity to the paths which the 'hunter' follows in search of the 'treasure' of their game. I introduced them directly to the rule of construction which David, Greg and Ian had investigated, but their work soon took on an unexpected and considerably analytic approach.

Fieldnotes: 5 December
... I explained that if their instructions (for 'finding the treasure') always stuck to a rule about how to change direction, then, if we use a repeating series of numbers, a pattern would emerge. I suggested the rule 'always turn right' and Julie and Louise

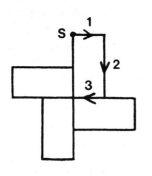

picked the numbers 1, 2, 3 to be the repeating series. I then showed how the pattern could be constructed using these numbers. Starting at S the first line is drawn one unit long, the second two, the third three, the fourth one, and so on.

They both immediately got the idea and set to work making various patterns using series with differing numbers of terms in them.... Every now and then Louise would say, 'Now I'm going to do an experiment to see if ...' or Julie, 'I wonder what would happen if....' Most of their patterns were constructed in response to a specific question they had raised. Sometimes similarities between patterns were noticed and then further investigated....

I then asked Julie what the pattern for '1' on its own would be. She soon drew this (a) and without further comment from me, proceeded to draw patterns (b), (c) and (d).

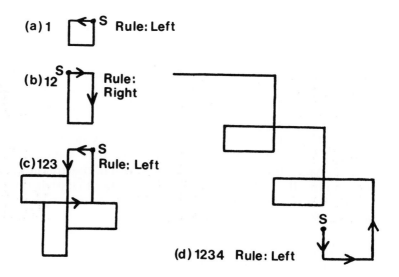

(a) 1 Rule: Left

(b) 12 Rule: Right

(c) 123 Rule: Left

(d) 1234 Rule: Left

She thus ordered her investigation so as to give insight into how these patterns grow from their simple origin. Indeed, she interpreted my initial suggestion as a starting point for this enquiry. From the above and the other patterns which she and Louise had made, she concluded that all series of four terms produced patterns which do not close. (I leave it to the reader to work out why and under what conditions Julie's hypothesis is true.)

She then made various patterns using 3, 4, 5 or 6 termed series. I then noticed that two of Julie's patterns (8,1,2) and (2,8,1) were identical. The three of us looked at this and soon realized (I think it was my suggestion) that if we keep repeating ...8 1 2 8 1 2 ... it is really the same as ... 2(8 1 2) 8 1.... The order of the numbers is, in a sense, retained (that is, they are cyclic transpositions).

While I worked elsewhere, Julie decided to look at this feature more closely. I did not realize at the time that she was going to do this, but when I returned, she showed me what she had done.

She explained how each pattern in (f) was a cyclic transformation of the others, and that the same was true for the

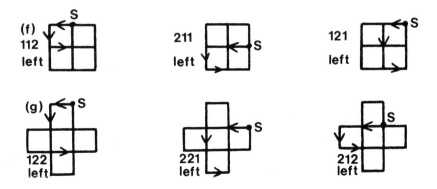

patterns in (g). She also said that there were no other ways of arranging the set (1,1,2) or the set (1,2,2). She went on to repeat the same idea using the set (3,3,4).

I then suggested she try the series (3,3,6), realizing that it should produce an enlarged version of (1,1,2). It did. Julie and Louise then compared (3,3,6) with (3,3,4) and (1,1,2) and tried to figure out why (3,3,6) and (1,1,2) were similar but (3,3,4) was different. After a little puzzling and no help from me Louise said, 'Look! in (1,1,2): 1 + 1 = 2 and in (3,3,6): 3 + 3 = 6: but in (3,3,4): 3 + 3 ≠ 4. So (1,1,2) and (3,3,6) are similar and (3,3,4) is different.' I reminded them of how yesterday they had demonstrated their Treasure Hunt game to me using fairy steps instead of paces. They saw the analogy between the (3) in (3,3,6) and the (1) in (1,1,2) on the one hand and paces and fairy steps on the other. Here there was scaling factor of 3. Listening to my explanation and recalling her own, Louise then said, 'But that's really the same as I said, isn't it?' Indeed, her explanation does imply a scaling factor and could not have been more logically expressed.

For much of the time Louise worked beside Julie, following her own enquiries and occasionally chatting about her findings. They both did many more patterns not recorded here. When they came to sort these out they noticed that they had both done a pattern for (3,2,1,6,7) but that their patterns were different whichever way up they were turned. They then noticed that while Louise had used a 'Right' rule, Julie had used 'Left'. I gave them a mirror and they saw that one pattern was a mirror image of the other. They then played a game imagining that one of them was the reflection of the other in an imaginary mirror. Every time Julie put out a left hand, Louise put out her right, and so on. They soon saw that there was a general rule something like this: 'If you change right for left it's like making a mirror image.' This explained the difference in their patterns.

Finally, they chose to sort their work out in a logical (rather than chronological) order and made it into a folder, 'So that I can show my Nan', said Louise.

I have since spent several hours making patterns using this kind of directional rule with the most satisfying results almost regardless of which numbers are chosen. But the striking feature of Julie's and Louise's work was that rather than make one pattern after another for the aesthetic satisfaction that this would provide, they soon became interested in analyzing their patterns, making hypotheses and considering the relationships between the number sequences involved.

They never attempted some of the more exotic patterns which David and Greg had worked on (for example, by using the series of integers from 1 to 10), but soon chose to work on the simpler ones which they could analyze with some success. When Julie chose to extend my initial suggestion by following the series (1) by (1,2), (1,2,3) and (1,2,3,4), she was not trying to make pleasant patterns, but attempting to understand their development. Again, by considering cyclic transpositions such as (1,1,2), (1,2,1) and (2,1,1), she was not expecting some dramatic pattern to emerge, but was testing the hypothesis that cyclic transpositions of a series produce identical patterns. For Louise, the question of mirror images, and her insightful remarks concerning the scaling factor between two patterns, all show the same analytic interest in her work. Finally, their decision to collect their patterns together in a logical order confirms this judgment.

This work has one distinctive feature in common with that of Ian's determining of the mid-point of his aeroplane wing, discussed earlier. Both were working at one stage removed from the concrete operations themselves. In Ian's case, the concrete operation was his centring-in measuring strategy; in Julie and Louise's it was the construction of patterns from rules. Their thinking was removed from these operations by virtue of the fact that in each case the results of the operations themselves were operated upon. Ian worked from the results of his measurements to gain a better position for his mid-point; Julie and Louise analyzed the rules themselves and constructed hypotheses concerning their relationship to emergent patterns.

It is interesting to compare the work of Ian, Julie and Louise (aged respectively 9.8, 11.1 and 10.4 at the time of their work) with aspects of Piaget's formal operational stage of development which is not considered to emerge before about 12 years old. Here is Flavell's interpretation of one aspect of this stage:

What is really achieved in the 7–11 year period is the organised cognition of objects and events per se (i.e. putting them into classes, seriating them, setting them into correspondence, etc.). The adolescent performs these first order operations, too, but he does something else besides, a necessary something which is precisely what renders his thought formal rather than concrete. He takes the results of these concrete operations, casts them in the form of propositions, and then proceeds to operate further upon them, i.e. make various kinds of logical connections between them (implication, conjunction, identity, disjunction, etc.). Formal operations, then, are really operations, performed upon results of prior concrete operations.[7]

One can see how the thinking of Ian, Julie and Louise in the work described foreshadows the type of adolescent thinking characterized by Piaget. For while they do not manipulate propositions within a clear logical framework, they do each operate upon the results of their concrete operations, and construct hypotheses which they seek to relate.

Making and testing hypotheses was a characteristic of much of the work in the classroom. The term 'hypothesize' in this context requires some examination. There is a weak or general sense of the word 'hypothesis' according to which most, if not all, knowledge acquired by an individual from the earliest ages is the result of the validation or refutation of some hypothesis. Thus an infant who utters, as one of his first words, 'want', might be said to be acting upon the 'hypothesis' that to make such a sound will result in the required object being placed before him. The validation of the 'hypothesis' contributes to his learning the application of the word. Popper goes further and asserts that any act of observation is loaded with expectations which presuppose hypotheses upon which such expectations are founded.[8]

But hypotheses such as these, while they may be a useful conception in epistemology, exist at a level which is largely unconscious and unarticulated. In much of their work in Chris Harris's class, the children constructed hypotheses in a much stronger and more specific sense. Predictive propositions were made, supported by argument and tested. The process of framing such hypotheses places the child at a stage removed from direct and concrete experience. It involves not only such questions as: 'What will happen if . . .?', which may be no more than an expression of curiosity, but also: 'Which of these possible explanations is the correct one? How can I discover this?' or 'What are the conditions under which this will apply?' Such questions are suggestive of an enquiry which is systematic and 'formal' in the Piagetian sense.

Jason, together with some friends, was examining a set of wheels fixed into axles which were mounted on a frame. Rubber bands were stretched between the wheels to provide a gearing system between the drive wheel of a steam engine and the wheels of a cart on which it was to be mounted. He was considering the speed of rotation of four of these wheels in relation to that of the drive wheel. He found that two of the four wheels (one large and one small), which were securely attached to either end of the same axle, both rotated once for every ten turns of the drive wheel. I then asked Jason why this should be so. These are the words in which he replied: 'Because the axle turns around at the same time as the big one. Both wheels are secure on to the axle. So both go round at ten.' Jason's reasoning is correct and displays the logical nature of a general hypothesis that wheels rigidly fixed to a rigid axle all rotate at the same rate. His clear expression of this reasoning, almost in the form of a syllogism, led me to suppose that he fully realized the self-evidence of his observation and the necessity of the truth of the general hypothesis.

However, the children went on to construct a different assembly of large and small wheels in the hope of providing a more effective gearing system. Again measurements were made of the relative speeds of the wheels. But this time, inaccuracies of which the children did not appear to be aware crept in, and from their measurements it appeared that two of the wheels which were fixed to the same axle in fact required differing numbers of rotations of the drive wheel in order to revolve one turn. The wheels were checked and found still to be secure on their axles. At this point Jason's comment was most significant. He said, 'How come they were the same before?' (that is, why, in our previous measurements, did wheels on the same axle rotate at the same speed?). He immediately added, 'We ought to check the first one again' (that is, re-take the readings with the first configuration of wheels). As it happened, working on suggestions made by others in the group, Jason did not do this but was able to eliminate the discrepancy by taking all measurements simultaneously. In this way he found his original hypothesis to have been correct after all.

The fact that Jason considered it necessary to check his earlier measurements confirms the interpretation of his previous reasoning as being a proposition of general application. It had not been an explanation only of this particular instance of wheels rotating at the same speed, but of all such wheels. Hence, in his view, the need to check in the light of apparently contradictory evidence. But if he saw his hypothesis as being self-evident and derived from logical deduction, as his explanation had suggested, why then did he now think it necessary to check it? Arguing along Piagetian lines, we should have to conclude that he saw the need to make the re-test because he was insufficiently certain of the necessity involved. Piaget claims that conclusions which will later be arrived at by logical deduction, and which indeed will come to seem quite self-evident, must in the beginning be checked against the evidence of what one finds by doing. Jason, so it would seem, is sufficiently advanced to make the deduction (or at least, to see the general and logical implications of the observed phenomena), but needs to return to practical experimentation since he has not reached a stage at which such knowledge is secure. While this explanation for Jason's desire to make a re-test is most plausible, the implication that he has therefore not reached some higher stage of development, and that his thinking is thus limited, is not at all clear. Such an example demonstrates his limited knowledge of the world but does not demonstrate a cognitive limitation. If Jason is working at the frontiers of his own knowledge, surely it is no weakness that he has to return to re-examine what had been conceived as self-evident.

In the case of the wheels and axles, Jason's reasoning is clear-cut and logical. But the children's investigations — and arguably those of adult scientists — often followed a more developmental path. As in the children's enquiries at Hoby Field Centre (described in Chapter 3), they would start with hunches, or even wild guesses, to explain the regularities or irregularities they observed, but then invent experiments to test out their hypotheses. It was this process from hunch to test results that interested me as Sarah investigated a problem arising from some dice-throwing.

Sarah had been doing some fairly routine work from a textbook introducing probability. It involved throwing dice and making estimates and tallies of the results. When I came to her she explained the work to me, and appeared to have some, albeit imprecise, notion of ratio or proportion. For example, she guessed that out of 100 tosses of a coin she would expect 'heads' to come up 50 times; and that from 600 throws of a dice she would expect 'about 100' sixes.

Fieldnotes: 8 January

I asked Sarah if there were any other questions which she could raise concerning the work so far. Phrasing my question thus vaguely, I was somewhat surprised by her perceptive response. After only a moment's thought, she said, 'I wonder if it makes any difference to the number that turns up on the dice which number shows when I start to roll it?' She explained how she had been rolling the dice off the palm of her hand. She wondered if it would make any difference to the result if, say, the number (1) was initially uppermost when the dice was on her hand. With virtually no assistance from me she went on to describe how this could be investigated experimentally. First, with (1) uppermost in her hand, she would roll the dice and record the 'score'. This would be repeated twenty-five times. (She initially said that sixty times would be better but that it would take too long.) She would then make a bar chart of the results. The experiment would then be repeated with 2,3,4,5, and 6 initially uppermost. By comparing the charts with what might be expected had she tossed the dice 'just anyhow' she would be able to see if the initial position affected the outcome.

Sarah followed this procedure and soon produced the first bar chart. (For the sake of economy, I reproduce her results here in the form of tables rather than bar charts.) Her first results, starting with (1) uppermost, were:

Face No.	Frequency
1	0
2	3
3	3
4	7
5	6
6	7

Having completed this, she examined the dice, noting that (1) and (6) appeared on opposite faces. With no prompting from me she suggested the following tentative hypotheses to explain her results:

(a) Since the frequency of (1) was zero, then, perhaps the initial face will not become uppermost in the final position of the dice.

(b) The face opposite the starting face (here 6) will always score high.

I asked her if she could offer any explanation for the initial face not turning up at all. She said: 'Because the dice would have to rotate completely round to end up in this position.' I replied: 'But don't you think there is enough space for it to make one complete turn? (It appeared to me that the dice, in rolling off her hand, had made at least one complete revolution.) She said: 'Yes, perhaps it does rotate once, but there's not enough space for it to go round twice.'

Her explanation seemed most plausible and not only accounted for the low frequency of the initial face, but also for the high frequency of the opposite face (face 6 scoring 7).

Sarah now went on to the second part of her experiment, repeating twenty-five rolls with face (2) initially uppermost. Her results were:

Face No.	Frequency
1	2
2	0
3	3
4	2
5	14
6	4

Sarah was delighted with this result. 'So we've proved my theory', she said. Indeed the results were even more convincing support of her hypotheses than the first set. Again the initial face scored zero, but this time the opposing face (5) 'won', scoring 14.

The experimenting continued, with her friend Nicola drawing up the graphs. But now everything started to go wrong. With initial face (3), (3) turned up three times instead of zero, though the opposing face (4) did score the highest. Then, with initial faces (4), (5) and (6) Sarah's hypotheses did not seem to fit at all. In each case the initial face scored at least as high as some other face, and in no case did the opposing face score highest.

By the end Sarah seemed understandably gloomy. However, she was prepared to re-examine all the results together. I asked her if she now thought that her 'theory' had been completely wrong. Had the first sets of results just been a 'fluke'? She replied that her 'theory' had been right for the first two sets of results but wrong for the last four. She was quite unprepared to go back on her explanation of the first two sets of results. She appeared to think that the conflicting results of the last four sets did not invalidate her hypotheses but rather that, for some reason of which she was unaware, the hypotheses were no longer applicable to these later results.

We did not pursue this question further as Sarah was keen to return to some other work.

Comparing this with the earlier example of Jason's work with the gearing wheels, it will be recalled that Jason had intended to carry out his initial experiment again in order to check his hypothesis concerning the rotation of wheels fixed to an axle, even though he initially perceived this hypotheses to be self-evident. Sarah, on the other hand, sees no reason to reject her original hypothesis in spite of its being highly conjectural. This refusal could be taken as demonstrating her weddedness to her original hypothesis: her refusal to give up what had seemed an appropriate explanation in the light of conflicting evidence. According to such an interpretation, she did not really see the truly hypothetical nature of her explanation and, having once elaborated it, perceived it as a rule concerning which there could be no degree of flexibility.

But such an interpretation seems most implausible in the light of the way in which she framed her hypothesis and supported it by considerably articulate argument. She was clearly impressed by the overwhelming support given to her hypothesis by the second stage of the experiment. The probability of such results following her prediction by mere chance alone is very small indeed and, although she had no way of calculating this 'level of significance', she no doubt intuited it to be of very considerable value. So, when she says that her hypothesis worked then but not now (rather than coming to the alternative conclusion that it was after all invalid, and that the results of the first and second experiments were merely 'fluke'), we can only take it to mean she considered the explanatory power of her hypothesis to be limited to the earlier experiments. In fact, the later conflicting results were produced after a considerable time had lapsed from the conclusion of the first two experiments (due to the morning break). Perhaps, when she renewed her experimenting she started with the dice in a higher or lower position in the palm of her hand, or perhaps it was rolled on to a different surface. Such a change in the experimental conditions would of course lead to results which conflict with those predicted by her hypotheses. Thus Sarah's insistence that her hypotheses worked then but not now appears to be thoroughly rational and does not suggest that she was unaware of their hypothetical nature, but only that their degree of generalizability was limited.

The important feature in the examples of both Jason's and Sarah's work is that they were able to make a predictive hypothesis, to support it by rational argument and to submit it to the test of further observations. The way they interpreted the results of such tests may at first sight appear somewhat naive, but is, upon further reflection, nonetheless scientific.

A fundamental feature of much scientific inquiry is its hypothetico-deductive character. Hypothetico-deductive reasoning goes one stage further than that evidenced in the work of Jason and Sarah. It involves the elimination of a hypothesis (or hypotheses) from a set of possible hypotheses. Flavell characterizes the general form of such a strategy thus: 'Well, it is clear from the data that A might be the necessary and sufficient condition for X, or that B might be, or that both together might be needed: my job is to test these possibilities in turn, to see which ones really hold true in this problem.'[9] The beginnings of even such a formal strategy as this, claimed by Piaget not to be developed until adolescence, were evident in the work of a few of the children in Chris Harris's class of 9-11-year-olds.

Of all the children in the class, David was perhaps the most interested in science. His considerable knowledge and skill, together with his general experience and familiarity with a broad range of scientific activities, enabled him to use his intellectual powers to the full in work of a scientific nature. This brief extract from the fieldnotes shows clearly his ability to use reasoning which is essentially hypothetico-deductive.

Fieldnotes: 16 October
David arrived at school this morning with a switch which his father had given him from a piece of electrical machinery he had been taking to pieces. The switch had three positions — off, half, full — and four electrical contacts.

David asked me how he should join up the contacts. I merely said that I thought he would need to have a wire leading from each contact. He said, 'Oh yes, that's two wires going to the battery and the other two going to the bulb.' (He obviously

intended to put the switch in circuit with a battery and bulb.)
He had soon arranged his circuit like this:

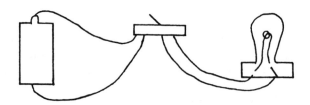

and showed me that the bulb could not be made to light up.

He said he thought that the battery may be no good. He explained how, if he joined up several batteries, then even if each one had insufficient power to light the bulb on its own, together they might be powerful enough. Since the batteries had been stored in a drawer for some time, this explanation seemed very reasonable.

He stacked two similar batteries on top of one another, joining them with sticky paper to ensure a sound contact. Reconnecting the circuit, he found that the bulb would still not light up.

He repeated the idea using six batteries that he had found in the drawer, joining them in a similar way. Still the bulb would not light up.

He explained that the switch might be faulty and so removed the switch. With all six batteries the bulb would still not light.

He then clearly stated that either the batteries were all completely dead, or the bulb was dead, and that all he needed was *either* a new battery *or* a new bulb in order to find out where the fault lay.

We then found a new battery. Using this (but no switch) David found the bulb would light. David now said that the batteries had been completely dead.

The switch was now introduced and the circuit worked perfectly.

In this brief experiment David postulated four hypotheses to account for the failure of the bulb to light.

H1   The batteries are too weak to power the bulb on their own, but will in conjunction.

H2   The switch does not work.

H3   The batteries are completely dead (that is, all six have insufficient power).

H4   The bulb does not work.

While he did not consider this set of possibilities at the outset, his strategy was systematic and hypothetico-deductive in several respects. He realized that there was no conclusive evidence for H1 on the basis of his tests with multiple batteries and that H2 was a possibility. He thus neutralized for the effect of H2 (by removing switch). He realized that this also provided no conclusive evidence for H1 in the light of the possibility of H4. He then suggested two alternative tests each of which would establish whether H4 or H3 was correct. After finding a new battery he was able to discover that, since the bulb lit up, H3 was correct and H4 and H1 were incorrect. Finally, by reintroducing the switch he established that H2 was incorrect. Such a strategy accounted for the possibility of various combinations of H1–H4 (for example, that both the switch and the bulb were not working, by not including the switch in the test after he had found a new battery). David's realization that either a new bulb or a new battery was required in order to solve the problem was correct. That he did not demand both clearly demonstrates his ability to use deductive reasoning and moreover his concern to view the activity as a scientific problem rather than simply directed towards fixing up a circuit in which his switch could work.

In these examples I have considered how the children framed, tested and eliminated hypotheses. But their scientific thinking involved more than these aspects. It also required an ability to conceive of and define problems whose solution they sought. In the previous chapter I described how their activities (or, in general, problems) gained a structure of increasing order and focus as a result of the children's interpretations of both their material environment and their responses to it. New problems arose as each phase of the work or intrusion upon it (by way of accidents, errors and so forth) was interpreted. In such a way the children's goals adapted to the changing circumstances brought about both by external conditions and by the process of the work itself. Where the work revolved around the construction of hypotheses for the solution of problems, the development of the children's goals and the problems raised by them was more clearly identifiable. More was involved than simply the solution to a given problem. For now the results of the tests conducted led not only to the confirming, rejecting or modifying of hypotheses framed for the purpose of solving the initial problem, but such results would themselves suggest further problems to be investigated and possibilities for their solution.

Such was the case when David arrived at school one morning and said to me: 'Can you make a candle burn under water?' Without waiting for a reply, he explained how this could be done by submerging a weighted container, with an air pipe attached, so that the candle could continue to 'breathe' under the water.

Fieldnotes: 16 January
David soon found the necessary materials for his experiment: rubber tube, candle, plasticine, and two plastic cylindrical containers. There then followed a series of experiments as David attempted to overcome the problems which arose, and to exploit the new possibilities.

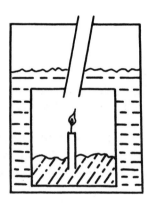

Diagram 1.

Experiment 1

The first problem was to see if the candle would stay alight once it was sealed — with an air pipe attached — into the inner container. We lit the candle, but when David put the lid on the container it went out. David explained this result as follows: when the candle burns it gives off carbon dioxide. This carbon dioxide is emitted from the tube, thus preventing more air from entering. His answer: we need two tubes, one to let out the carbon dioxide and another to let in more air. (This reasoning was purely his own, as were all the explanations involved in the work. While he did at times ask for points of technical detail, he arrived at his own conclusions. This result had not, however, been predicted by him though one or two other children in the class had said it would not work because the candle would not get enough air.)

David thus prepared his materials for his second experiment.

Diagram 2.

Experiment 2

One tube would let carbon dioxide out, the other, air in (Diagram 2). David did not explain which would do which. Again, the candle was extinguished when the lid was closed.

David was at first puzzled by this. I started a discussion on how hot air rises (he was very familiar with this idea) and further suggested it might help if one of the tubes was inserted near the container's base.

Immediately, David saw that this would help and went on to explain how (an explanation which he repeated to me at the conclusion of his experiment). He said that it would now be like a pump, with air being sucked in through the bottom hole while carbon dioxide was pumped out of the top hole. Thus David assembled this third experiment, borrowing my drill again to make the necessary holes.

Experiment 3

The candle was lit and the top of the container placed. Again the candle went out. David puzzled over this, then suggested that not enough air was getting in. It would be better, at this stage, he said, to remove the tubes altogether to see if it would work then.

Experiment 4

This time, at last, without the tubes, the candle remained alight. But David's excitement was somewhat dampened when he saw what else was happening. The lid around the hole above the candle was melting, thus expanding the hole. The hole quickly grew until there was soon little lid left.

David said that the problem now was that the plastic lid was too near the candle flame. We needed a larger container so that the flame would not melt the lid around the hole. I suggested a plastic bucket upturned — a dispensible paint container about twenty-five centimetres high. David drilled a hole at the top for the 'carbon dioxide' to escape and another near the rim for the air to enter. I suggested there might be a problem of air entering between the rim of the upturned bucket and the table top. So we placed the bucket on a large plate of water to effect a seal around the rim (my idea).

Experiment 5

Much to David's surprise the bucket around the top hole again began to melt as the candle burnt. He had not realized that the candle's heat would be so intense at this distance.

After some thought he said that this time he should use a different material that would not melt. He suggested — and found in a junk box — an old tinned food can with the lid removed. Holes were drilled in this in the same manner as before.

Experiment 6

This time the candle was snuffed out when the tin was placed over it. David thought that this was because the top of the tin was too close to the flame and thus acted as a snuffer to the candle. He suggested how this could be overcome by using two tins fitted together — one of them having the bottom as well as the top removed — so as to form one long tin. I gave David considerable help in fitting two tins together in this way by crimping in one of the tins so that it fitted into the other. A hole was drilled into the top of the upper tin, but David forgot to drill one at the bottom of the lower tin.

Experiment 7

In spite of their being no hole at the bottom the candle stayed alight. David explained his success here by saying that some air was getting in at the join of the two tins, thus allowing the circulation. I'm sure this explanation is correct.

By now, David had set aside his original idea of getting a candle to burn under water. He was more interested in exploring the possibilities of a candle burning within a container. While in most respects he was satisfied with his last experiment, he was unhappy about the fact that the light of the candle could not be observed through the tin. In this respect plastic was a more satisfactory material. He now saw his aim as that of making a lamp — a candle burning within a translucent container.

Returning to the idea of using plastic, David described his next experiment. If he were to place an upturned tin on top of a plastic tube of similar diameter, the plastic tube would let the light through, while the tin on top would not melt. With this plan in mind we searched the school for an appropriate tube and eventually found a yellow translucent plastic tube thirty cen- timetres high and eight in diameter. David drilled four holes near the bottom of this (he reckoned that one might not let in enough air) and on top placed a tin with a hole drilled in its top (see Diagram 3.)

Experiment 8

This worked beautifully, giving a warm, yellow glow. David delighted in demonstrating how the light could be dimmed by partially covering the inlet holes, or extinguished by completely blocking them.

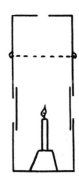

Diagram 3.

Several children came to admire David's lamp. We then took it off to a dark room where he again showed us how he could dim or extinguish the light.

David had invented the hurricane lamp. Unfortunately, there was not enough wind outside to give it a good test. Perhaps he will try that later. After he had allowed the lamp to burn for some fifteen minutes he extinguished it and removed the tin lid. Beneath this the plastic had become very soft and was beginning to melt. David took this opportunity to explore the possibilities of a partly melted tube by moulding it with his hands into some abstract sculpture. Later in the day this idea was taken up by several children who used bits of candle and tubing to produce distorted, gnarled shapes. They also explored the sooty deposit from the candle flame — scratching it, writing on it, making fingerprints from it and so on.

But David, after a brief diversion on this, wanted to return to his lamp. It was not quite right yet. The top of the sides of the tube must also be of tin so that they would not melt. However, the part of the tube adjacent to the flame could be of plastic since this part had not begun to melt and indeed did not even get hot.

David puzzled over how this might be done. I contributed little except to remark that the only part of the lamp that really needed to be translucent would be that part near the candle flame. I suggested that we just look through boxes of junk material. Perhaps we would spot something that would give us an idea about how to construct the next lamp.

As luck would have it, after very little searching David found a sheet of clear acetate (the kind used to cover spotlights, but this was not coloured). He soon decided how this could be used, rolled into a cylindrical shape and inserted between the two tins of Experiment 7 and a further tin. Thus the lamp tube now consisted of a tin cylinder at the base, then a band of acetate sheeting, and above this two joined cylinders, the top one having a hole drilled in its lid.

David raised the candle on a platform so that the flame stood adjacent to the clear acetate sheeting. No inlet holes were made, David explaining that as constructed there were sufficient gaps between the acetate sheet and the tins to allow air to enter.

Experiment 9

The lamp worked perfectly. Though now David had no method of controlling the light by blocking air inlets, the light cast by the lamp was much brighter.

Here this stage of experimenting ended. David went on to investigate melting plastic and melting candle wax and crayons, making his own coloured candles out of crayons and string. The lamp was taken apart so that he could use his candle for this new departure in his experimenting. The lamp itself meant little to David as an object. He was not concerned to keep it. He was even prepared to melt his only piece of acetate sheeting 'to see what would happen'. That this would ruin his lamp was of little concern to him. He had done what he wanted to, and was well satisfied with his experiments. The product of his labours, the lamp, was of trivial significance compared to the process which he had gone through and which he intended to continue, albeit on a slightly different track.

Later today, however, after David had spent some time on these other experiments, he did return to me to say that he preferred plastic to tin as a material and that he was now going to work on a revised version of the lamp, to be made from two clay cylinders and a coloured plastic tube. He liked the coloured light this gave even if it was less intense. He is now waiting for his clay tubes (made by forming clay around a plastic tube and then withdrawing it while still wet) to dry.

Here David's experiments were conducted according to certain hypotheses which became more refined as consecutive results of the experiments were analyzed and accounted for. David saw that in order to make a candle burn under water, the main problem was to find a way in which it could burn within a sealed container. The first seven experiments worked towards the solution of this problem. Although I offered a hint by reminding him of the idea that hot air rises, David almost immediately suggested the analogue of a pump which, together with his knowledge that a candle needs air to burn and gives off carbon dioxide, provided the clue for solving the problem. But David then turned his attention towards making a lamp. He saw that this presented further problems concerning the translucence of plastic and non-melting of materials. His further brief investigations (a series of activities involving softened plastic, candles, soot, etc.) were seen as offering all kinds of possibilities which were followed up during the week or so after the lamp experiments. David's concern primarily for the actual process of investigation itself, rather than the making of a lamp (which he was prepared to destroy in pursuit of further investigations), demonstrates that he was working primarily as a problem solver (and to that extent a scientist) rather than as a technician. His divergent strategy, covering a wide range of scientific aspects (combustion, circulation, light, melting properties, etc.), allowed David to relate the results of his experiments to a broad area of his previous experience. In this way his 'scientific' concerns (and those of the others who became involved in this work) were continually being related to those of his more 'everyday' life, thus imbuing the scientific knowledge he gained with significance, meaning and reality.

An essential feature of David's activity was his control over it. Without this, the various paths which he followed would not have emerged in a way which was so appropriate to his knowledge, interests and so on. No teacher (let alone work card) could have predicted these paths or determined ones so appropriate for his growing scientific skills.

Notes

1 RUSSELL, B. (1946) *History of Western Philosophy*, p. 570.
2 PIAGET, J. (1964) *Six Psychological Studies*, p. 61.
3 See, for example, DONALDSON, M. (1978) *Children's Minds*, especially Chapter 4. See also, ZAPOROZHETS, A.V. *et al.* (1971) 'Development of thinking', published in *The Psychology of the Pre-school Child*, ELKONIN and ZAPOROZHETS (Eds), p. 233.
4 GARDNER, D.E.M. (1969) *Susan Isaacs: The First Biography*, p. 68.
5 ARMSTRONG, M. *op. cit.*, p. 11.
6 VYGOTSKY, L.S. (1962) *Thought and Action*, p. 83.
7 FLAVELL, J.H. (1963) *The Developmental Psychology of Jean Piaget*, p. 205.
8 POPPER, K. (1972) *Objective Knowledge — An Evolutionary Approach.*
9 *Op. cit.*, p. 205.

Chapter 5

Representation

In Chapter 3 I showed how the children's control over their work consisted in their ability actively to interpret and reinterpret it. In this way they gave meaning to it which ensured that its structure became more clearly ordered and that new perspectives on it emerged. In the last chapter I showed how part of this attempt by the children required them to stand back from their immediate experience and to abstract from it. They grappled not only with the direct experience itself but also with the rules, hypotheses and systems they invented to explain it. What I now want to explore is the role that writing plays in this process.

Michael Armstrong had shown how many of the children he studied were concerned with the forms of written and artistic expression they used.[1] Like adult artists and writers, he argued, children appear to have a concern for the formal qualities of their work. To what extent, I wondered, was this concern for form part of the process by which children stand back from their direct experience and make it external to themselves, in order that they may thereby more deeply understand it?

A characteristic of Greg's working style was that he would, during the course of investigative work, stop at regular intervals to sort out what he had done, to prepare it for presentation and to write little pieces describing what had taken place. Perhaps these activities were more important to him than to any other child in the class. He certainly needed no encouragement to write about and present his work in a meticulous way. This is how he wrote after I had been in the class for just a week. He had been spending much of the previous three days working with some narrow wooden triangles, making polygons, considering angles and constructing patterns.

Fieldnotes: 6 September
Greg soon started writing:

> TRIANGLES   Wednesday September 6th
> On Thursday last week when we were walking into P.E.
> Mr. Rowland

He then stopped and said to me, 'What are you? Are you our helper?' I explained that I was hoping to help the children in the class but also wanted to find out about how they learn. He wondered whether, in his writing, he should refer to me as 'our helper' or 'another teacher'. He questioned me as to why I was helping and trying to find out about the children. I said that I could be called a researcher and tried to explain what this meant. He said he had heard the word before but hadn't understood it.

Later in the day, without further assistance from me or Chris, he showed me his finished writing.

> On Thursday last week when we were walking into P.E. Mr. Rowland our Researcher told Me, David Pacey and Jason Sewell that we could make some good models with this wood that was on the workbench so when I was changed from P.E. I got 36 pieces and made a circle putting all the right angles together and all the non right angles together then on the following Monday I painted them 6 green, six red, six black, 6 yellow, six blue, six white when they were dry I built some patterns and then I put them away.

This is a perfectly accurate account of what happened. Greg attaches importance to the numerical precision and the details about how the 'circle' (36-sided polygon) was constructed. He needs to have me 'defined', not only for the sake of knowing what I am doing, but also so that I can be 'named' and 'categorized'. His recollection of how the work was initiated by my suggestion that the children 'could make some good models' was, as far as I can remember, word perfect.

Greg chose to write in a similarly precise way when he wrote the few sentences beneath his matrix of Fibonnaci Series (see p. 32). He was also capable of writing in an expressive style in his story writing. But in his accounts of his work he kept to precise reporting or even bits of instructions.

As well as writing such accounts, Greg would often spend hours preparing his work for display, sorting out his materials, tidying up his folders and so on. On such occasions he would often be cheerful, even exuberant. There were times when he would sing at the top of his voice as he mounted a picture here, and then there, to achieve a desired effect. I would often attempt to restrain such excitement, not only because of the disturbance he was causing (unintentionally, I think) to the other children, but because I felt that his almost obsessive arranging and re-arranging had little to do with the intellectual content of the work itself.

I was at first inclined to view such activity in purely social terms. Perhaps this was Greg's way of attracting attention to himself. Or perhaps such obsessive sorting and arranging reflected some kind of need for security. Maybe there was some truth in explanations of this sort. But as I reflected more upon the results of such excitable activity I began to interpret it as not so much a diversion from the real task at hand as a kind of period of consolidation. There were interludes in the work of many of the children when they would step back from their work, 'play' with it and chatter not too seriously about it. It was during such episodes that their work became more really their own, was placed in a more social and everyday context and was understood more deeply by them. This kind of explanation seemed particularly justified in Greg's case since, following such light-hearted interludes, he was invariably able to give a rigorous account of his different pieces of work and how they related to each other.

If my interpretation is right here, we may view Greg's concern for display not so much as a presentation of his work, but as a representation of it. Through such activity he recapitulates, summarizes and orders his past experience. The displaying and organizing activity is as much part of this as the writing.

While Greg often appeared to place great value on other people seeing his displays, this was not, I believe, their main purpose. His friend David appeared less concerned to display his work for the benefit of others, but nonetheless he also liked to write about it and draw diagrams relating to activities that he had previously completed. He had a little exercise book in which, quite unprompted by Chris Harris or myself, he would do this writing and drawing. In this book his style of writing was precise, even instructional. It was almost like a textbook on geometrical techniques. But in spite of this predominantly 'social' mode of language (with its suggested awareness of audience) it was an almost private book, one which he was prepared to show me but which was not written with the intention of showing it to anyone. The book was a series of 'displays', like Greg's, but displays for which he considered himself to be the chief observer.

Fieldnotes: 22 March
On the second page he took up the '6-petals in a circle' motif which had been experimented with by Dean and others. This, in reduced size, is what was on this and the following two pages.

1 This pattern was made
  like this

2   First you draw a circle like this one

3   and then you put your compass point on the edge of the circle and you shode get something like as shown

4   Then at the end of the semey circle you put your compass point and you shode land up with something like this

5   Keep doing that till it looks like this

What is in one sense an analysis of the task done is also an instruction and a kind of 'pondering' over the elements of the task.... It is very similar in appearance to much of Greg's displays, and is perhaps influenced by Greg indirectly. (This was altogether David's idea, but he often works with Greg and has no doubt considered Greg's approach to such tasks.) But where Greg intends his instructions to be displayed, David puts his into a book where he knows that few will look. Clearly this was done for his own benefit as was largely the case with Greg also, it is just that the display provides the context for this analysis or contemplation of the elements of a task. In the above example David knows full well how to make a petal design and would be unlikely to forget. Nevertheless, by contemplating the stages in its construction he is enabled more deeply to understand it. If this is the case with Greg also (as I suspect it is), it accounts for why so long is spent in redrawing or rewriting his work for display. It has been apparent that after such display activity Greg invariably appears to have a keener appreciation of his work.

Greg's and David's pieces of writing, and the activities which went with them, may be seen as consolidating their previous experience and as objectifying it, that is, making it external to themselves. The style of writing, with its attention to detail, reflects the nature of the experiences which they represented. But they do not go beyond the experiences themselves. Their effectiveness lies in the extent to which they re-create and report on the work which preceded them; they were not intended to go beyond this work, to explore new relationships, to relate the work to other experiences.

The kind of writing that the children did in conjunction with their visits to Hoby Field Centre (described in Chapter 3) was of quite a different nature. These trips evoked in the children feelings and thoughts which were less well organized than those evoked by the mathematical experiences described above. The area of land we explored, with its locks, weir, ruined bridge and so forth, gave one a sense of the social history, the natural history and the geography of the place. While such feelings were expressed and developed by the children's preparedness to invent explanations and to formulate and test hypotheses which arose from their observations, it was through writing that some of the children were best able to capture this feeling.

Helen and Karen had made drawings of the Old Bridge at the centre. It was Chris Harris's suggestion that they (together with others who had shown an interest in the bridge) might like to write something about it. Before writing they informally discussed the bridge, exchanging experiences and observations. From the wide range of types of writing that followed, it would seem that while this discussion got the children thinking, it in no way determined the content of the writing which followed.

Fieldnotes: 26 September
Helen had spent much of the morning of our last visit to Hoby

underneath the bridge. She had been very excited about various pieces of the old broken pottery and glass bottles which she had found on the bed of the canal stream under the bridge. She had also fallen into the stream. (A small stream was all that flowed along the bed of the original canal at this point.)

She wrote this:

> The Old Bridge
> The Old old bridge,
> now it is deserted old
> and creepy. Brocken glass
> and pottery. Still dirty
> black water chickweed still
> and green, silent now is
> the old old bridge much
> different than 100 years
> ago at least.

In the margin beside the poem were drawn simple pictures of the following items, each labelled accordingly, and headed, 'things you would find in a brook or old canal', a broken cup, broken bottle, slashed picture, potty, broken alarm clock, cracked jug.

What Helen has written here is no doubt a precise account of her experience. But it is more than that. She had put together her experiences under the bridge and related them to the bridge itself. Her finds and the observations of the stream give the bridge a historical perspective.

Helen's poetic style adds to this, 'Still dirty black water chickweed still and green' is a fine sentence, the repetition of 'still' giving a sense of both lack of movement and permanence through the ages. 'Silent now is the old old bridge' is an effective inversion, appropriate to the form of the poem and contrasting well with the more usual grammatical order of the first two lines: 'The old old bridge now it is deserted.'

But while her style here is highly successful, the piece does not give the impression of being sophisticated. The bridge is 'old and creepy' and 'Much different than 100 years ago at least', both phrases which she would use in her everyday language. She told me that she had been told that the bridge was probably built aroung 1810 and it was therefore more than 100 years old. 'But', she said, 'it is really "about" 100 years old isn't it?' While it is a poem, Helen is concerned not to write anything which is inaccurate.

The little drawings around the poem do not show the things that she in fact found. There is no illustration of the old tin pot or the cracked mirror which she did find; but several things, such as the potty and the alarm clock, which she had not found, are drawn in the margin. In drawing these 'things you would find in a brook or canal' she has allowed her imagination to take her beyond her actual experiences towards a general idea of the kind of things that you might find. This contrasts with the very particular experience which the poem relates.

Helen here integrates her experiences under the bridge in such a way as to express a feeling of the effect of the passage of time on the present. Karen, in this next piece, expands upon her experience in a different way. For her it provides the opportunity for speculation about the existence of the bridge through time.

Fieldnotes: 27 September
While Helen was writing her piece on the Old Bridge, Karen was also writing. I did not see her work until it was finished, then she showed me:

Old Bridge
The old bridge at hoby stands weak and still, the canal runs under the bridge while the old dead tree leans against it. Each day that bridge gets older and older its about 200 years old now. The bridges bricks wear out more each day. The wind takes the bricks right out the bridge. They crash to the ground. One day when a storms high and mighty the old bridge might not be there.

This piece contrasts with Helen's in several ways. While Helen's interest was with its being 'deserted' (see first sentence), Karen is concerned with its being 'weak'. They both explore these ideas in relation to the bridge's history. But Karen does not use her experience of the bridge to conjure up a feeling of its history by relating her experience, but rather speculates upon that experience. She contemplates the bridge's passage through time ('each day that bridge gets older.... One day when ....') both past and future, whereas Helen concentrates on the present and how this is affected by the past. They thus explore different aspects of 'historical experience'.

In order to conceive of this passage through time, Karen has had to take a step back from her immediate experience and to reflect upon it. How did the bricks become worn? What will happen to them? The present itself becomes of limited significance, being only one part of the bridge's life from beginning to its final destruction. Karen explained to me afterwards how wind and rain would gradually wear down the bricks just a little each day, and how one day they would become so weakened that they would be blown out.

Considering the writing as a piece of poetry or prose, Karen was not very pleased with it. She did not like 'stands weak and still', though having talked to me about it after she had finished the writing, I think it was a good way of expressing what she had in mind. She also didn't like 'The wind take the bricks right out the bridge.' It was not the missing 'of' that concerned her. It was rather her inability (as she saw it) to think of a word that would describe the way in which the wind would remove a loosened brick. 'Blows over', 'blows down' or 'blows out' do not seem to describe the brick's motion appropriately (apart from being rather mundane expressions) and yet 'takes (the bricks) right out', while describing the motion of the bricks did not, for Karen, seem to go with 'the wind'. I see the problem she has, but in fact rather like the way she has decided to express the idea.

The last sentence, 'One day when a storm's high and mighty the old bridge might not be there', is excellent. Her switch from present to conditional tense is just right. (A classic example of a usage which is not accidental, but neither is it 'intentional' in the sense of 'a conscious use of a device intended to have a specific effect'.)

The final understatement, 'the old bridge might not be there', while poetically providing a contrast with the 'high and mighty' storm, fits in with her way of conceiving of the bridge's history. The bridge is at the mercy of nature's intervention through time; its destruction is just another event in its history.

James Britton suggests a rough definition of literature as being 'the written language in the role of the spectator', adding that the shaping of experiences 'typically takes place as we go back over our experience in the role of spectators.'[2] It is clear that Helen and Karen are 'shaping their experience' through their writings. But in both cases they go beyond their immediate experience of the bridge. There is a parallel here between the way in which Karen and Helen 'shaped' or 'operated upon' their experience of the bridge, and the way Ian 'operated upon' his measurements made to find the mid-point of the aeroplane's wing (see p. 71). In both cases, a step is taken back from the immediate experience itself in order that it may be reflected upon.

But most of the children's writing was not reflective to this extent. Often they would write in recollection of some past event — a holiday, bonfire night, Christmas and so on — or in anticipation of it. The aspects of recollection and anticipation would often be closely interwoven, the object of the writing perhaps being to capture the excitement of the occasion, an excitement which is at once particular to the individual child and yet common to the experience of them all.

However, I have often been disappointed by the attempts of children to write about those experiences which, in conversation, they recall with such liveliness. Why is this liveliness so rarely transferred from the spoken to the written word? But my disappointment resulted from a misunderstanding about the difference between writing and talking, differences to which Michael Armstrong alluded in his analysis of the children's writing in my own class.[3] When they write, children (like adults) are forced to consider the formal problems, be it a matter of spelling or the clear sequencing of ideas in the development of an argument. They thus have to stop and consider not only what to say, but how to say it. This being the case, their ability to write in such a way as to 'bring to life' the events they describe is an activity requiring them at once to stand apart from these events (that is, the recollections or imaginations of them) and at the same time to project themselves back into them. Looked at in this way, what surprises one is not so much the fact that children find this task difficult, but that they are indeed able to tackle it from such an early age.

It is in this light, I believe, that we should consider the following piece of writing by Jason, in anticipation of Christmas Day:

Fieldnotes: 7 December

Christmas

On Christmas day you get so excited and your dying to open your presents. I slide down the banister and I land in my dads tool box. Then I get up and loosen the door then take steps back then I run and bash into the door then I charge at my gifts then I sit on them I say I think I've squashed them.

This little piece certainly reflects Jason's sense of humour. At first sight it sounds very much like something Jason would say when talking about his excitement at Christmas. Yet, looking closer, it is quite different from anything he, or anyone, would actually say. Certainly, in conversation, no one would use the ending Jason uses: 'I say I think I've squashed them.' The first sentence would also sound somewhat artificial when spoken. I asked Jason to read his ending to me. From his reading of it, it seemed to be consciously ambivalent. On the one hand it refers to him áctually saying, within the narrated sequence, 'I think I've squashed them'; on the other hand it stands as a reflection upon the sequence of events made from outside the narrative itself — a kind of epilogue. Both interpretations seem appropriate in their humour and in their moralizing implications — 'If you get too excited you're bound to muck things up!'

On first reading I had thought that Jason's shift from second person in the first sentence to first person in the rest was wrong. Now it seems obvious that this is not the case. The opening sentence is a generalized statement — many adults might use 'one' instead of 'you' here. The general statement tells us what the piece is going to be about. The shift to the first person then becomes necessary because it would have been perverse or senseless to relate such a lively and individual account in the second person. His account, while capturing the essence of getting 'so excited' (with its physical high spirits and resulting disaster) does so by describing a particular and personal experience (who else would land up in their dad's tool box if they slid down the bannister?), but one with which we can readily identify.

Jason's attention to the detail about how he loosens the door first, then take steps back, before bashing into the door not only makes the scene vivid, but adds to our understanding of his particular type of excitement. It is an excitement which is not completely abandoned; he has enough self-control to loosen the door first. (Jason demonstrated this action to me after he had written the piece.) But in spite of this element of control to his excitement, he still ends up squashing the presents.

I have suggested that it is a difficult task to re-create past experience through writing in a way which captures the liveliness of that experience. Jason's piece to a large extent succeeds and, as far as I could ascertain from the conversations I overheard between Jason and his friends while he wrote the piece, the talk directly contributed little to the writing. However, on other occasions, talk and writing were integrated as a child, or a group of children, went over their past experience and put form to it. If the act of writing itself distances children from their experiences, then perhaps there are times when talking can help them to project themselves back into these experiences. The talk and the writing may then become an integrated activity, the one aspect of which can only be understood in relation to the other. This is not to say that on such occasions the writing is a mere copy of what is said. On the contrary, its form is totally different.

For Dean writing was often an essentially social activity. As he wrote he would show his writing to his friend (usually William or Jason), talk about the subject matter and at times about the way he should write. The conversation would often be full of excitement as Dean 'lived out' the recollections or imaginary events that his writing described. But the writing itself usually lacked this quality. Perhaps this was because of the difficulties involved in transferring the atmosphere of the events from a spoken form to an appropriate written form. But perhaps also this was because he did not see the purpose of the writing as we might see it. Like several of the children in the class, the judgments he made about his own writing seemed to show a concern not so much for evoking an atmosphere which reflects how he responds to the events (as Jason so successfully did in his 'Christmas' piece), but for an accurate and systematic account of events which are themselves of intrinsic interest (to Dean, at least).

Fieldnotes: 31 January
Prior to this writing Dean had become very involved in the drawing of house plans. He had made several plan drawings of his own house, some of these being done at school, others with his father's help at home. Having spent most of two or three days on this drawing, he decided (quite on his own) to write a piece which would be called 'My Home'. He thought a while and then wrote:

My Home

I was born in my house. . . .

Here he stopped and could not think of what to write about. He and William discussed how William had been born in a hospital whereas Dean had been born at home. Their conversation soon led on to their early childhood: 'I had an old bike which . . .', 'Do you remember my go-kart?' and so on. They have known each other as long as they can remember.

After they had chatted a while, Dean resumed his writing. Now the writing and talking went hand in hand. Dean would write about his scooter, then talk to William about it. Their conversation naturally led on to the next episode in their lives and Dean would start writing about that. The events talked and written about followed a chronological sequence from Dean's earliest memories and what he had been told about his baby-hood. They all related to the theme of Dean's various modes of transport, as if projecting backwards to his birth his current obsession for cars and bikes. He was no longer concerned with 'My Home' as such but rather 'My Life' in terms of his present interests.

Meanwhile William wrote little, if anything, but paid great attention to what Dean was writing. The writing seemed to be a kind of record of the conversation. Or was it the other way round? Perhaps the writing offered some structure — the detail by detail chronological account of Dean's bikes, scooters and go-karts — which determined the course of the conversation. . . .

When Dean finished the writing he read it over to me. I asked him some rather general questions and he pointed out several places where he wanted to change what he had written. . . .

Over the next day he rewrote the piece twice. The changes he made were not the direct result of my criticisms though in most cases he told William and myself why he had made the changes. Here is a composite version of what he wrote. In this, words in round brackets were part of the original writing which were excluded from the final version; words in italics appeared in the final version but not in the original; and words in square brackets are clarifications I have added. The final version is untitled.

> I was born in my (house) *bungalow* and *when I was one* I had a pushchair and now the bottom of my pushchair is a trailer for my go kart and it is yellow and the top of my pushchair (is at) *went to* the tip and when I was a bit older I got a scooter and then a bike (I learnt to ride my bike. First) it had staples [stabilizers] on and then my Dad took them off and I could ride *it* and then I bust my scooter and that went down to the tip and my Bike had a hooter and my brother Kevin sat on my bike and the spokes shoot [shot] out and the wheel came off and then I had a go-kart and nothing happened to that because I have still got it and then I had *a bike* a tomahawk *and that is all rusty* and then *I had* a chopper [another brand of bicycle] (and my chopper is in good nik because it is in my garage and I am going to go on it tonight) *and that is silver and I have to clean it because it is mucky*.

Dean explained most of his changes to me. 'House' was changed to 'bungalow' for the sake of accuracy. He explained how 'when I was one' needed to be added because, without it, it sounded as though he had a push chair as soon as he was born which was not the case. He changed 'the top of the push-chair is at the tip' to 'the top of the push-chair went to the tip' as a result of conversations with William from which he guessed that it would probably not still be there and so his former version would be inaccurate. 'I learnt to ride my bike' was omitted because, he said, he could not really ride it until after the stabilizers were removed. He did not explain the final changes to me, but I guess that he added 'a bike' before 'a tomahawk' because I had asked him what a Tomahawk was; 'and that is all rusty' explains the fate of the Tomahawk which is otherwise left open; and the change of the final sentence fits in more with the theme of the piece.

Dean was pleased with this writing. He felt he had 'got it right' and that he now had before him a clear sequence of the events which interested him. However, as a piece of prose one might readily criticize it. It communicates little of Dean's reaction to the events: his excitement at getting a new bicycle or his dismay at its being broken. It appears much like a catalogue of events through which the individuality of the writer barely emerges. While one might account for such weaknesses in terms of Dean's limited technique, it is important to view the writing not simply on its own but within the context of the talk that accompanied it. The talk provided the 'life' of the activity of recollecting and exchanging experience, the writing provided its logical structure. That Dean did not transfer the vividness of his conversations with William to his writing was not only because of the difficulties he would have had in doing this, but also, in part at least, because he did not see the need to make this transference.

But even for Dean there were occasions when he would choose to write without talking to the friend who sat next to him. One very snowy morning, some two weeks after he had written his piece about his life, this is what Dean wrote, while sitting quietly next to his friend Jason who was also writing:

> Today it was snowing and I got up and I opened the back door it was up to the window me and my dad cleared it away it was about 3 ft. down near the back door my go-kart was coved with snow I went in I had my coco krispies and went back out and had a look at my bike it had a bit of snow on it because [of] the holes in the garage door [where] the snow had blown in and I cleaned my bike I went in and got my bag and went to schol and it was deep and I went in and it was swimming [i.e. the class were due to go for a swimming lesson) so I went back out to wait for William he came and we played out for a bit and then went in. We had to go to Mrs. Atkin because Mr. Harris was not here there was no swimming then Mr. Harris came and I had my milk it was frozen and then did my picture and then I rot about snow.

What is of interest here is that Dean chose not to talk with Jason about the snow which concerned both of them in their writing (nor, it would seem, did they read each other's work until they had finished). While this piece resembles the last in relating to a sequence of events which are worked through one at a time, the differences are revealing. Whereas a sequence of clauses or sentences are, in the first piece, joined together by 'and' in every instance except one, in this writing there is a more definite sentence structure with clauses appropriately joined together but at other times being separated into sentences (though Dean does not actually punctuate sentence divisions with full-stops and capitals.) The writing is much more fluent and less laboured, with the inclusion of many little details bringing the piece to life in a way which was lacking in the earlier writing. In the first piece the problem of shaping such a wide range of loosely related experiences extended over time was considerable. It was therefore not surprising that talk was needed in order to aid this process. The writing then provided a form to, and a record of, this shaping. But in this second piece, the experience related was already relatively unified and so the shaping was less of a problem and could be achieved by writing alone. Now Dean naturally expressed himself through writing, rather than talking, and it was this that resulted in the increased effectiveness of his writing style.

Comparisons such as this raise a fundamental question concerning the role of writing in the classroom. Under what circumstances is writing (as opposed to talking, painting, modelling, etc.) the most appropriate medium for children to express and/or sort out their ideas and experiences? The preceding examples suggest that, whatever the nature of the relationship between talking, writing and experience, children may have considerable ability to ascribe appropriate roles to talk and writing in the shaping of their own experiences. Greg and David needed to write, draw diagrams and make displays to this end. Dean, in the first piece, needed primarily to talk and in the second to write. What seemed to have been important in each case was that the child was permitted, and indeed encouraged, to work in a way which allowed him the freedom to adopt an appropriate balance among writing, talking, drawing or displaying as a means of representing his ideas.

In the children's accounts I have considered so far, they were concerned to portray their experience with precision and accuracy. On the other hand, in their story writing children are freer to use their imagination to interweave fantasy into their more everyday experience. Perhaps then, a clearer understanding of the ways in which fantasy and experience are related in their stories might shed more light upon the relationship between writing and experience.

To pursue this idea, I shall follow a sequence of stories by Jason and Dean, partly because their previous work has served to introduce them and partly because of the contrast between their writing styles.

The stories by Dean probably represent his first attempts to evoke an atmosphere through his story writing. Prior to these, his most successful writings had been factual accounts. His stories tended to consist of routine plots, often concerning car chases and robberies. As with his writing about his bicycles related earlier, the talk that accompanied his writing appeared to be of more significance than the writing itself, though he usually enjoyed the writing and talking activity and needed no persuading in order to write.

When Dean approach me saying that he wanted to write, but was uncertain of a theme for a story, I saw this as an opportunity for helping him out of what appeared to be a rut in his story writing.

Fieldnotes: 3 April
... I thus suggested he wrote about getting lost in a forest. I then told him the kind of thing that could happen. Perhaps he would find a lake, and as the weather became dark and stormy he would meet an old man.... I chatted on and Dean became absorbed in my story as I improvised it. He seemed attracted to the kind of story I had in mind.

I envisaged that Dean would go on to make up his own story following the same theme. I was thus pleasantly surprised when he came up with his own idea. He said, 'My story's going to be about an old barn. It will be all dark and spookey and there will be haystacks flying about the barn. It's going to be good.'

As a title for his story Dean wrote 'The Old Farm Yard', and said that he could start like this: 'One day I was bored and I decided to go down to the farmyard.'

I replied, 'Couldn't you miss out the first few words and just start "I went down to the farmyard"?'

Dean said, 'No, that wouldn't be right.' He then thought a moment and suggested another opening. 'I went to the farmyard to get some chickens' eggs.'

Dean clearly saw that the opening sentence had to set a context for the story. At its most basic, this context may be provided by 'One day' (or 'Once upon a time' if it is to be a fairy tale). He seemed to understand my point about 'One day' being redundant, but was insistent that a realistic reason should be given for his going to the farmyard in the first place.

He started to write, confidently and with few pauses:

> the old Farm yard
> I was going down a old farm yard I was going to get some eggs for my mum and I went in to the Barn to look for the chickens but they were not there....

Here Dean turned the page, saying, 'This is going to be good, this is!' and continued:

> .... I thought they was here yesterday I looked all over for them. I went back home and told my mum my mum said I wonder where they went. The farmer must of put them some wherer....

I interrupted to say, 'When are you getting to the bit about the haystacks blowing around?' Dean replied, 'Next, I'm going back to the barn. The chickens are on top of the hay and I look for a ladder. It's going to be good!' He continued;

> ... so I said to my mum I will go back down there after dinner. I had my dinner, and I said to my mum I will be off now so she said take care I was walking down Park Lane and I saw the Farmer with the chickens so I ran to the Farm I got in the barn and I saw the chickens up on a hay stack I thought that if I got a ladder I could get up to the chickens so I was going down a old dusde [dusty] barn and hay stacks (were) blowing around the barn it was scarey I ran a man caught me I was pulling and pulling I got a way I ran as fast as a car

Dean liked the simile 'as fast as a car'. He said he really wanted to end here but was not sure if it was 'right'. I said that this seemed an appropriate place to end if he had nothing more to say.

The only other conversation between us concerned three or four spellings. The writing had taken about fifty minutes.

Dean thoroughly enjoyed writing this story and was delighted with the result. Throughout, he was concerned with the structure of the story, not only the beginning and end, but also where his original idea, which was to be the climax of the story, should fit in. His enjoyment seemed to consist in the anticipation and setting up of this climax.

In this last respect Dean's writing resembled much of the writing of children of his age. Often in their factual or imaginary narratives many little everyday details are recounted before the climax is reached. While such details may often appear to be boring and irrelevant to the reader, they represent the child's attempt to relate an extraordinary experience, fantasy or germinal idea to the world of everyday experience. Opening gambits, such as 'One day', are further devices which children use to categorize and place their imaginings, and Dean's insistence that he should have a reason for going down to the farmyard again shows his need to relate an imagined story to the realities of life.

Nevertheless, although he has been very concerned to make this relationship, he has to a large extent failed. (But this is not surprising since it is probably one of his first attempts to write in this way.) For while up to the climax in his story the narrative flows relatively smoothly, there is then a sudden jump into the world of 'scarey' fantasy: 'If I got a ladder I could get up to the chickens so I was going down an old dusty barn and haystacks were blowing around. . . .' This shift reduces the story's credibility: we are not led convincingly up to the climax. But it is nevertheless clear that Dean was concerned that we should be led up to the climax in a realistic way.

The morning after Dean wrote 'The Old Farmyard' he was joined by Jason. Although I had expressed an interest in Dean's story, I had not mentioned any of the above points.

Fieldnotes: 4 April
Dean recalled our previous day's talking about getting lost in a forest. He again wanted to include his scene of 'Haystacks blowing about in the wind'. Jason was also attracted to this strangely evocative idea. They discussed the possibility of men attacking them in the forest and how the men could be ravaged by eagles. Together they enthused about the wild life they might find in the forest.

I played no part in the writing which was done enthusiastically and at top speed. When, at one point, I did ask Dean what had happened in his story so far, he replied, 'You'll have to wait until I've finished.'

This is what Dean wrote. Several grammatical mistakes are, I believe, merely due to the speed with which he wrote.

> I was walking in a dark forest and hay stacks [were] blowing a round and mice crawling and rats crawling and birds roosting in the tree tops and piking food like worms out of the ground and bats flying around and I saw a fox and some dogs and I was frightened and cows going moo and I was looking over the little bit over [of] grass I saw two men and a nother two and a nother four and I was worried. I saw a little rabbit and I looked up the sun was out some eagles came down and got one of the men it eat him up and I was walking along and I saw a pond and alligators and crocodiles came at me I ran the golden eagle went at the back of the crocodile and killed it and I was not worried now because the golden eagle was on my side and it flew away buy this time my mum wondered where I was my brother came on his Dt 175 YAMAHA and he came pulling wheelies and he said you have got a motor bike at home waiting for you so I ran home and it was there my Xt 80 and I said to my dad will you put my Xt 80 in your boot please yes take me down to the forest please yes said my Dad I get my helmet I put all my stuff on and went trailing.

(Dean told me yesterday that he hoped for a Yamaha Xt 80

motor bike next Christmas. He would use the bike for trailing and it would fit into the boot of his father's car.)

In this story Dean no longer sees the need for a lead in. Instead he builds on his original idea, no doubt stimulated by his conversations with Jason. But it is most important that, in spite of his ability to get straight to the 'climax', he still needs, in the latter part of the story, to relate the fantasy back to his own reality. In this story it is the details about his motor bike, rather than the sequence about collecting eggs from the chickens, which provides the realistic context for the fantasy. Dean makes the switch back to reality thus: ' . . . by this time my mum wondered where I was. . . .' This is an ingenious device which plays the same role within the narrative as some of the formulae which other children use, usually at the end of their stories, for example: 'I woke up and it was all a dream.' This switch marks the beginning of the end of Dean's story. Together with the preceding sentence where he realizes that the eagle is, after all 'on my side,' it resolves the problem of how he is going to emerge from the nightmare world. His final return to the forest to ride his motor bike confirms that the frightening experiences have now, in effect, vanished in the realistic light of day.

While Dean was writing his story, Jason also wrote. Jason's story opens with a similar scene involving the haystacks blowing around and the description of the wild life which they had discussed in their preliminary conversations.

I was walking down a dark forest which was going down a hill with haystacks blowing around with adders wriggling under them and harvest mice crawling and common brown rats crawling and sparrows roosting and owls hooting and bats squealing and echoing as they fly I was on my own and frightened as the mist rose I noticed that squirrels and rabbits were out and birds were singing in the early morning sun and as it was getting late I soon realised that I should be going on my way and I went through the rest of the forest I was getting tired because I didn't have any sleep I was still walking and just like that I fell to the ground asleep when I woke up I soon ran fast then I came to this pond and I jumped in and I sank to the bottom and I floated again it was clean fresh water so I filled my bottle up and a crocodile was kreeping behind me and I was lucky to have steel toe caps on I went for a dive and my feet went up and hit him in the face and it knocked its teeth out when I got out I let my clothes dry when they were dry I got on my way as I was walking I saw a flock of starlings and there were so many the sky was black for 7 mins. as though there was an eclipse I was nearly there now as

nightfall fell it was cold and misty and I was frightened when
sunrise occured I got on my way by dinner time I was there
and Id just finished my last can of beans
The End

Jason has considerably more familiarity with this kind of writing
and many of his pieces (like, for example, the short Christmas piece
noted earlier) succeed in evoking an atmosphere by relating individual details. Here he confronts the same problem as Dean, a
problem which emerges from their joint discussion. The way he
tackles it makes an interesting contrast. He excludes the rather wild
details of the men chasing him and being ravaged by eagles. Such
extravagance is excluded on the grounds of realism and he does not
allow himself to get carried away as does Dean. Jason uses more
subtle devices, such as the flock of starlings blacking out the sun, to
produce an altogether more dramatic effect. In this way he reduces
the problem of relating his fantasy to reality: there is less that requires
explanation. Jason's resolution of the fantasy in the last sentence, 'by
dinner time I was there and I'd just finished my last can of beans',
neatly adds a domestic touch sufficient to put the nightmare behind
him in a way which does not reduce the narrative's plausibility. In
such ways it is clear that Jason has gone some way toward solving the
literary and imaginative problem which beset Dean. He is able to
represent his imaginings plausibly, to relate his fantasy with due
regard to the constraints of reality.

It should be emphasized that my purpose in comparing the
stories of Dean and Jason here is not to pass judgment on the
relative 'value' of their work, but rather to highlight the concern
which they both have in their writing for relating fantasy to reality,
how this affects the structure of the story and leads to a greater
control over their imaginative powers. For it is this relationship
between fantasy and reality which gives a story its meaning. To get it
'right', to make the fantasy plausible and to give it significance
present a challenge for the child writer. They also present a challenge
for the adult novelist. It is, perhaps, partly through their successive
attempts to meet this challenge that children learn not only how to
write, but also how to bring their imagination under control and
sharpen it as a tool for thinking.

But closer parallels than this can be drawn between the writing
of the children in the classroom and professional adult writers. The
novel is one means by which adults explore the perennial problems of
the human condition: problems of personal freedom the relationship
between the individual and society, the fragility of human relationships and so on. But such concerns appear to have roots which
stretch back well into childhood. Children conceive of such problems

in a different way and use different literary forms and devices in their exploration of them. Many of the children's stories which, on first reading appeared to be merely expressions of childish innocence and simplicity, on further reading appeared to reflect a concern for problems of more fundamental and human significance. I am not suggesting that the children in Chris Harris's class would often write stories with the conscious intention of exploring some aspect of the human predicament. This is rarely the case with successful adult novelists and would be most unusual for a child. But it appears that in the process of writing, just as children are drawn to relate fantasy with reality, so they are also drawn towards these deeper problems. The permanence of the written story and the deliberation involved in its creation by its nature demands that the writer reflects upon such matters as the reasons for the actions which take place and their implications. What has impressed me is the way in which children appear to meet this challenge.

This process often becomes very apparent when children puzzle over what is going to happen next in their stories. As each event is followed by the next and explained in terms of it, problems arise which require some resolution. These problems may then become the focus of the story as the characters within it begin, in a sense, to take on a life of their own.

One can see how this happens in these next two stories by Laraine. While she began to write with little idea of where it would lead her, she soon became very involved in the problem of the possessiveness and fragility of human relationships and the individual's underlying solitude. Through the stories she seeks to resolve this.

Fieldnotes: 15 November
I came across Laraine towards the end of the afternoon. She was starting a story. Beside her was a picture from a set of picture cards made up by Chris Harris to be used as an occasional stimulus for writing. The picture showed a sailing schooner by a quayside. The quayside was deserted except for an old man sitting on an upturned box. He was smoking a clay pipe, with a bottle and glass of whisky at his side. The sun was setting over the sea. . . .

I asked her if she could tell me what was going to happen. She replied that she didn't know yet but would find out as she went along.

She worked rapidly, stopping only occasionally to hear about the problems her friend Karen was having with her sewing. I sat with her quietly during most of the writing, and, by the end of the afternoon, she had finished.

The Sailer and his Stories
This story is called, The baby Seal.
Long ago said the sailer to the little boy I was on my
boat called the 'Merry Man.' All of a sudden I could here
a little noise. So I looked around and saw a little baby
seal, looking at me and with his little black eyes he
looked so sad and unhappy that I picked him up and took
him to my little hut on the boat. I gave him my last drop
of milk and a little bit of fish that I caught that day. We
got on so well together that he stayed with me for 4 days
on the fifth day we went ashore to get some food. All so
we got some fresh fist for the baby seal. When I got back
to the boat I called the seal because it was dinner time.
No seal came So I called again, again no seal. So I looked
around the boat Still no seal. I was so upset that I went to
my hut. When I opened the door a hole lot of seals
jumped on me. So you have found your friends. But
there was no ansew. So off they went all in a line. I think
they are all happy now.
the end

The little boy, to whom Laraine's sailor tells his story, is not in
the picture. When I asked her about this she said that really he
was not telling his story to a little boy at all, he was just 'going
over it in his mind'.

When she had finished the piece, I asked her at what stage
had she thought up the ending. She replied that she had stopped
to think for a long time after 'Still no seal' before realizing what
the ending would be. . . .

On reading the piece over in the classroom I was particularly struck by the ending. The man's being 'upset' at not finding
the seal, followed by his disappointment at the seal not answer-
ing his 'So you have found your friends', then the transformation
into a happy ending. Talking this part over with Laraine, it was
quite clear that she intended the man to feel first this sorrow and
then also the gladness that the seal would now be happy. One is
left with a feeling not so much of sorrow suddenly transformed
into unequivocal gladness, but rather with a kind of 'coming-to-
terms' with the two feelings — sorrow at losing the seal plus
gladness at his happiness — as is demanded by the realization of
the seal's right to freedom. 'So you have found your friends' is
the 'philosophical' state of mind in resolution of the conflict.

The style of this last section fits in clearly with that of the
rest of the story. The emotions are underplayed, particularly in
the short sentences 'No seal came. So I called again. Again no

seal. So I looked around the boat. Still no seal.' The subject is not treated with the kind of sentiment which so often accompanies stories written for children concerning these feelings. While this lack of sentiment fits with the 'philosophical' outcome of the story, it is also consistent with the context in which it is set. A hardened old sailor is likely to tell stories and to reflect upon his experiences with wisdom gained from these experiences rather than by an appeal to sentiment.

Laraine's writing was initially stimulated by a picture. The climate of this picture was one of solitude and reminiscence. She absorbs this climate and soon becomes involved in considering the essentially solitary nature of the sailor's life (or, perhaps, of life in general). Where a relationship with another being begins to form, the sailor realizes that he must control his own possessiveness. Laraine did not set out to tackle this problem but, as the story developed, she was led to consider these fundamental aspects of human relationships and does so with considerable skill and insight.

A week later she returned to write another story to her series, 'The sailor and his stories'. She did not relate this second story to a picture, but continued the theme of the first. I was not with her while she wrote.

Fieldnotes: 21 November

> The Sailer and his stories
> this story is called The Mermaid
> long ago, when I was on my boat called the Merry Man I thought I would go to land to get some food. When I was coming back from land I thought I would go to the rocky beach to watch the children play so off I went. When I got there it was nice and quiet. Soon it was time to go home but as I was walking home I saw a face behind a stone. I went to have a look to see what it was and I saw a mermaid. Hello I said. hello said the mermaid and off she went. Two days later I went to the same beach to see if the mermaid was still there. When I looked I saw no mermaid. but when I looked again I saw her. Sitting on the sand coming her hair with a fish bone come. Her tail looked so pretty in the sun. Because she looked so pretty, I went up to the mermaid and said you look pretty sitting there in the sun. The mermaid gave her hair one more come and went back in the water. The sailer has never seen the mermaid sinse.
> the end

... Laraine said she preferred the first story to this one, especially the end of the first story where the man feels sad to lose his seal yet happy that it will now be with its friends. I asked her if there was any way she could change or add to this story. She was certain that there was not.

My first impression was that this story did not somehow live up to the first. But on reading it over, its style does fit in with that of the first. Both stories are very credibly about the same sailor. They both relate his disappointment at being unable to make a sustained relationship, in the first case with a seal, now with a mermaid. Each story presents the problem as a 'fact of life' without dwelling on the sadness it causes. Laraine told me how in each story the sailor ended up feeling sad (but in the first one glad as well) but the way she expressed this seemed to reflect her feeling ' ... but that's life.' Here this 'philosophical' stance is confirmed in the final sentence which, with its shift from the first to the third person, acts as an epilogue to the story.

This second story does develop the idea of inability to sustain a relationship further than the first. Whereas the sailor did initially make quite a close relationship with the seal by taking him aboard and feeding him, contact is barely made with the mermaid; '"Hello", said the mermaid, and off she went.' But even this contact is sufficient to arouse hopes in the sailor of a relationship: 'I went to the same beach to see if she was there.' His disappointment is increased by seeing her combing her hair so prettily, and by his final approach to her which is rejected: 'I went up to the mermaid and said, "You look pretty, sitting there in the sun." The mermaid gave her hair one more comb and went back in the water.' Even the final 'one more comb' seems to be another signal, or symbol, of her rejection of him.

Laraine also told me how the sailor would often think of his past, now that he was retired and no longer sailed, and how he would have liked to be young again. This fits in also with his going to the beach, in the second story, 'to watch the children play'.

In these two stories Laraine has created a character through whose eyes she considers the world of human relationships and thereby tackles an issue of significance to us all. In this way her concerns are identical to those of adult novelists who, through their portrayal of human life, increase our understanding of it.

A theme that has run throughout my discussion of the children's writing in this chapter has been the way in which the act of writing creates a certain distance between the writer and the experience portrayed. This theme is taken up by Margaret Donaldson, who emphasized that the two critical features of the written word — its enduring quality and its relative freedom from non-linguistic context — encourage not only an awareness of language but also an awareness of one's own thinking which promotes the development of intellectual self-control.[4] My interpretation of much of the writing from Chris Harris's class suggests that through their writing the children would objectify their experience, thus casting it in a form which enabled them to view it critically, to relate it to their more general experience of the world, to go beyond it or, in general, to 'operate upon' their experience.

In the previous chapter, it appeared that the children's ability to 'operate upon' their experience was the key to their abstract thinking. The process of abstracting itself required this. The argument of this chapter is, then, that writing must play a crucial role in the development of abstract thought. Furthermore, through the narrative of their story writing, their thoughts were directed towards a continuous and critical appraisal, as the elements of fantasy and reality were related and the human issues which emerged were explored. It makes sense to view this kind of awareness on the part of child writers as enabling them to gain a degree of control over their imagination. And, if the imagination is the source of the intellect, they thereby gain intellectual self-control.

But while this attempt to exert a controlling influence — over their environment, their work and even their own intellect — is the challenge with which the learning child is confronted, there remains a central issue which I have not yet explored. That is, how does growth itself take place? It is a common observation that children appear to grow intellectually in quantum steps. There appear to be growing points, after periods of apparent consolidation, from which skills take a leap forward. How do these leaps forward occur? What takes children away from working in an area or in a way in which they can operate successfully, into more difficult territory where their abilities will be stretched? What is the relationship between the emergence, practice and development of a skill on the one hand and its creative use on the other? These are the questions to which I shall now turn.

Notes

1 ARMSTRONG, M. *op. cit.* Chapters 2 and 3.
2 BRITTON, J. (1972) *Words in a World*, in JONES, A. and MULFORD, J. (Eds), *Children Using Language*, p. 36.
3 ARMSTRONG, M. *op. cit.*, p. 11.
4 DONALDSON, M. (1978) *Children's Minds*, Chapter 8.

Chapter 6

Points of Growth

It should by now be clear that the children in Chris Harris's class were given every opportunity to be inventive and that, like most young children, they enjoyed inventing games rules and strategies. In much of the work I have discussed, where the children invented the rules which they followed, the path to their mastery was, in principle at least, clear enough.

But convention is as important an aspect of learning as invention. Where the rules of the work are conventional rather than invented (as, for example, in spelling, certain numerical procedures or the sonnet form of poetry), then the problem arises as to how children become masters of the rules they use rather than their servants.

Such a problem arose for Laraine. She had chosen an arithmetic computation card and was on her own, working in a concentrated fashion. When I approached her she asked me for help. By way of offering it, I began to ask her further questions. Soon we put aside the work card and she seemed happy to accept the way in which I now largely directed her work.

Fieldnotes: 20 October (cont.)

... First I asked her to do these sums.

(1)   29   (2)   48
      + 34   + 55
      ─────   ─────
      6 $\not{3}_1$ 3   10 $\not{9}_1$ 3

Which she completed as shown. Her procedure was:

(a) Add 'tens' (5 in (1); 9 in (2))

(b) Add 'units' writing down the unit of this sub total and 'carrying' the ten.

(c) Adjust 'tens' figure to account for 'carried' ten.

She was quite happy with this procedure and did not see the final readjustment of the 'tens' figure as the correction of an error. Indeed her method, while more circuitous than the conventional 'units' then 'tens' method (since the latter would have involved no alteration to the 'tens' sum), was in one way more logical since it dealt first with the more important figures. (Chris Harris notes here: 'Laraine can never have been taught this method. She seems to have rejected her teaching for a method that suits her.')

I then asked her further questions relating to the additions of single figures she had done within these calculations. While her replies were spoken, she expressed herself very clearly in a way that may be accurately represented by the sequences below.

(1a) $9 + 4 \rightarrow 10 + 4 - 1 \rightarrow 14 - 1 \rightarrow 13$

(2a) $8 + 5 \rightarrow 10 + 5 - 2 \rightarrow 15 - 2 \rightarrow 13$

(2b) $4 + 5 \rightarrow 10 - 1 \rightarrow 9$

I then asked her (3): $9 - 2$.

She said she did not have to 'work this out', she 'knew' it was 7.

and (4): $13 - 7$

She said that $14 - 7 = 7$ because $7 + 7 = 14$ and so $13 - 7 = 6$.

So far, Laraine had no problems. Her overall strategy in (1) and (2) is, if not completely original, at least one which she has worked out for herself. In dealing with single figures, her reasoning is clear, in each case (except (3) which she 'knows') reducing a problem which she does not 'know' (cannot solve by immediate recall of a number bond) to one which she does. My concern was, how would her reasoning be effected when she was on slightly less familiar ground? Would her approach still be one of reducing a problem which she could not immediately solve into one (or a series of ones) which she could? We continued. . . .

Fieldnotes: 20 October (cont.)

(5)   _56   No problem. Tens first again

      21

      ——

      35

Then   (6)   _42

      25

      ——

      23

I made no comment that this was incorrect, proceeding to the next question, which I wrote adjacent to (6) on her worksheet.

(7)   _48

      25

      ——

      23

I then asked her to look carefully at her answers to (6) and (7). Immediately, she said they could not both be correct. She then rechecked her working and said that they were, however, both right. I asked her if she was quite sure about this. She replied:

'Yes, they must both be correct because I haven't made a mistake.'

Many children follow Laraine's mistaken rule in this kind of calculation. But what is interesting here is that her following of the 'rule' takes precedence over the logic of the situation, a logic which she demonstrates that she is well aware of by immediately saying that (6) and (7) cannot both be right. It appears that the correct following of a rule is the sole criterion for the correctness of the solution. I was not sure to what extent the purely numerical nature of this work, divorced from any more real context, might have affected Laraine's reasoning. So we talked about going shopping and made up a 'story' which we illustrated with a diagram.

Fieldnotes: 20 October (cont.)

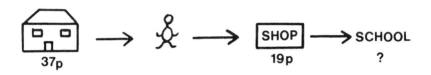

'You leave home with 37p in your pocket. On the way to school you spend 19p. How much money do you have when you arrive at school?' Laraine quickly said that she would arrive at school with 22p, showing me that she had 'worked it out in her head' like this:

$$(8) \quad \begin{array}{r} \_37 \\ 19 \\ \hline 22 \\ \hline \end{array}$$

When I repeated the story again, but replacing the 19p spent by 15p she again wrote out a 'sum':

$$(9) \quad \begin{array}{r} \_37 \\ 15 \\ \hline 22 \\ \hline \end{array}$$

I drew her attention to the fact that although she had spent less money in the second case, she still had the same money on arriving at school. She said that she thought this did not seem right, but after checking her working out, reaffirmed that she thought both answers were correct. . . .

Laraine went on to use play money to help her solve similar problems. She then found that, in response to a question like (8), she got one answer when she did it as a 'sum' and another when she did it with the money. Seeing this discrepancy, she said: 'They're both the same money but different answers. It can't happen. The sum must be wrong.' But she didn't see how. After much more work together with the money she gained some understanding of her difficulties and eventually explored new 'rules' for subtracting.

Such a sequence of events must be very familiar to any primary school teacher. But underlying the activity there are questionable assumptions about the nature of mathematical skill and its development. Laraine is an articulate child who is capable of working in a very logical way. Her apparently illogical strategy in this work stemmed from the way she perceived the activity she was involved in and the skills to which it was directed. The work was structured by my controlling influence rather than hers. Moreover, the activity itself was seen as being directed towards a skill divorced from any interesting context. She was 'well motivated' throughout, but motivation was not here sufficient. As long as the numerical skill was seen as something divorced from real life, then the logic which she readily applied to real situations was no longer operative. All that mattered to her, initially, was that she had correctly performed the process, or followed the rule. The fact that this was in fact a 'wrong' rule was fortunate since it eventually led her to re-examine her approach. Had she initially followed a 'right' rule she may well have solved her problems without ever confronting the logical nature of what she was doing. Her readiness to reduce the 'story' versions of the problem to a 'sum' demonstrates that she saw the 'story' as being only another way of illustrating the formal problem (which, of course, it was) rather than a problem of any intrinsic interest, and thus its solution fell foul of the same mistaken procedure. Eventually, working with concrete materials, she confronted her contradictions. But the problem then became one of translating concrete operations into formal ones. At this point, if the argument of Chapter 4 that children of this age can work at a considerable level of abstraction is correct, one should not be too ready to assume that this translation is incompatible with her 'stage of development.' As suggested before, what matters here is perhaps not so much the level of abstraction involved as the meaningfulness of the context from which *the child* makes the abstraction. And this depends upon the degree of control which the child has over the activity.

But while Laraine worked in a context which, initially at least, was inappropriate to the development of her mathematical skill because it was divorced from any meaningful context, it does not follow that children always develop skills merely as a matter of course in the pursuit of their own objectives. Indeed, it often appeared that the children would reach points in their activities where they would choose temporarily to set aside their overall objectives and enjoy an interlude in which they practise some highly specific skill. In David and Greg's work on Fibonacci series, discussed in Chapter 2 (see p. 32) we saw how David, on the second day of this work, went off on his own to practise the arithmetical skills involved in making number series. He did this because he had become aware of his difficulty and realized that it could be overcome by practice and that his mastery of this skill would enable him to control the activity. Far from being divorced from the aims of the activity *he* saw such practice as being necessary for its achievement.

My opening remarks to this chapter allude to a possible conflict, or at least a tension, between the mastery of conventions on the one hand, and inventiveness on the other. But it is the mutually supportive roles that inventing and learning conventions play that I want to stress.

In her initial calculations where she was adding numbers together, Laraine was certainly being inventive. It was in the later subtraction problems that her inventiveness was replaced by a 'blind' following of misunderstood rules, a blindness which resulted largely from her lack of control of the context in which she was using her mathematical skills.

In many of the mathematical activities with which I became involved, it appeared that a key feature of the children's mathematical inventiveness was their ability to reduce a task of some complexity into one which could be handled within the limits of their mathematical skill. It was often the case that such inventiveness was a vital preparation for the development of a new skill or technique. In this next example Dean prepares the ground for a future development of skills in multiplication.

Fieldnotes: 28 February
Dean, Jason and I had been talking about large numbers. Dean asked if there were any numbers bigger than a million and Jason explained how no number was the largest. Their interest led them to tackle two problems: how many millimetre squares are there on a large sheet of graph paper; and how many squares in the maths exercise book. Dean worked on the latter problem

while Jason worked on the former. This is how Dean worked. Saying that he would first need to count the squares on one page, he counted the number of rows (29) and columns (22). He said he would have to write down 22 twenty-nine times and add them together. But this, he said would be too difficult. I suggested grouping them into sets, but did not explain why or how big the sets might be. Without assistance he then drew this diagram on rough paper, explaining that he was grouping the 22s into sets of four.

```
        22                          24
        22    8       8             24
     80 22    8       8   24        10
        22    8       8             ——
        22            8             58

        22            8
        22    8       8
     80 22    8       8   24        240
        22            8             240
                                    100
        22            8             ——
        22    8       8   10        580
     80 22    8       2
        22
```

```
        22            80        Each subset consisted of 80 and 8. 20 and
        22    8       80   240  2 remained.
     80 22    8       80
        22

        22            80        He then put the 8s into sets of three with
        22    8       80   240  a set of ten remaining.
     80 22    8       80
        22

        22            80        The 'units' total was then found by adding
        22    8       20   100  the totals of the sets of 8.
     80 22    8
        22

        22                      A similar procedure was adopted for
        22    8                 finding the total of the 'tens'.
     80 22    8
        22

     20 22   2
```

He was left with the sum 580–58 being the number of squares on one page. Delighted with his method so far, he said, 'We're really getting somewhere now.' He began this sum in the conventional way, adding the units first

$0 + 8 = 8$ but when it came to the tens
$8 + 5 = 13$ he was unsure of what to do with the 13.

First he wrote the 13 in the 'tens column', then he said that he should only put down the 1 and 'carry' the 3; or was it put down the 3 and 'carry' the 1? He could not remember. I suggested that if he was unsure, he might think of his own way of doing it.

He thought a moment and then said, 'I know. I'll chop off the 500 and add the 80 and 58 and then add the 500 again.'

He wrote:

```
5 80
  58
─────
6̸138
```

and so he had 638 squares on each page.

He then counted that there were forty-eight pages in the book and said that he would have to write down 638 forty-eight times. Not deterred by the length of this task, he proceeded, using a similar strategy of repeated groupings and adding as before. But this time his 638s were grouped into nine groups of five, with a remaining group of three 638s. This is how he dealt with the remaining group:

638	adding 8s together	24
638	adding 30s together	90
638	adding 600s together	1800

Then, adding each column of the final sum he arrived at 181104. (The 110 is here the sum of two and nine tens which he realizes is 110, but does not see as eleven tens, ten of which need to be 'carried' to the hundreds). Immediately, he said this looked wrong and then, 'I know what. I'll do the 90 and 24 in my head and then add it to the 1800', and so he arrived at

```
  1800
+
   114
─────
  1914
```
with no need to carry...

The rest of Dean's calculating followed similar lines. Each time he was faced with a 'carrying' problem he invented some way of getting around it.

From this work, Dean's limitations in computational technique are very apparent. But what was remarkable about it was his ability to reduce a problem which seemed at first to be beyond him to an orderly sequence of steps which he could manage. Dean justly felt very proud of his achievement. Mathematical ability consists in a complex of skills of differing orders. While he had little command of some of the technical details, he showed considerable mastery in developing a strategy which is both highly systematic and appropriate to his level of knowledge and experience. There would seem to be good reasons for suggesting that this ability is the more 'basic' (in the sense of being fundamentally important to the growth of mathematical understanding) than the techniques which are often termed 'basic skills' of numeracy. Indeed, when it comes to the kind of analysis that is involved in computer programming, this ability to break down a complex task into a series of small steps is perhaps the most fundamental of skills.

Talking over his work later with Jason (who by now had also solved the same problem in a different way), Dean remarked that his own method had been very lengthy and it would greatly help if he knew his multiplication tables. Having pushed his present skills to their limit, he seemed to have gained an awareness of what skills or techniques he now needed, the fundamental condition for his gaining them. (Working over a similar problem some months later, he showed me that he had now come a long way towards mastering his tables.)

Theories of education (in common with much of art criticism in general) are commonly based upon a conceptual distinction made between 'creativity' and 'technique'. For example, Bennett assumed that teachers would emphasize one, rather than the other, of these aspects in their language teaching.[1] 'Formal methods' are said to emphasize the techniques of the so-called 'basic skills', whereas 'informal methods' are commonly seen as being more directed towards 'creative ability'. (Whether they succeed in achieving these supposedly diverse objectives is another matter and one which Bennett disputed.) This distinction is very apparent in much of the commercially produced teaching material. Those who adhere to the distinction are rarely able to describe in any but the most vague terms what is meant by 'creativity'. But if, by 'creativity', is meant inventiveness, then the argument I am trying to develop here is that inventiveness and the development of technique (which requires the mastery of conventions) cannot so easily be separated. No doubt children readily learn various tricks in order to get the right answers in their work cards or to guess what is in the teacher's mind, but it appears that the development of techniques which can be applied to real and novel situations is largely developed from activity within such situations.

Such an argument is often more readily accepted in regard to writing than it is with mathematical work. Mathematics, it is argued, is a hierarchically organized complex of skills and concepts which must be mastered in a more-or-less determined order. No one can do long multiplication before they can add. Thus, so the argument goes, activities must be externally structured in order that the skills and concepts are encountered and practised in the correct order. This necessitates taking control of the activity out of the child's hands and often divorcing the practice of such skills from activity of intrinsic interest. But while mathematical knowledge does consist of a logically related, and to some degree sequential, series of concepts, its concepts are multi-faceted. They can be approached by different routes and can be understood at different levels of abstraction and complexity. Thus, for example, the concept 'number' can at one level be grasped by a child in the infant class, but on another level remained a puzzle to Frege and later Russell at the height of their philosophical careers. The growth of mathematical understanding is perhaps not to be conceived in terms of a linear progression but as a loosely determined path through a multi-dimensional lattice of concepts which are mastered as existing knowledge is viewed from a new and more enlightened perspective. This does not contradict the view, now commonly held, that arithmetic and pure mathematics generally is nothing but a prolongation of deductive logic.[2] The sequence in which mathematical concepts are encountered and (to varying degrees) mastered does not necessarily follow the same sequence as that in which they are logically related.

This point is perhaps well illustrated by another piece of Dean's mathematical work. Completed only some three months after his struggle to count the squares in a maths exercise book, Dean still had only a cursory knowledge of the techniques of addition and subtraction, and had very little familiarity with multiplication or division. Yet he was able to grasp some of the basic concepts and skills relating to fractions, through this activity.

Dean had been working for several days on some caterpillars he had collected. (Some of this work was described in Chapter 2.) Now he had become interested in measuring one of his caterpillars which had shed its skin in order to study the rate at which it grew.

Fieldnotes: 12 June
... I then suggested we weigh the caterpillar. Dean said that if we used the classroom scales 'it would weigh nothing.' I asked if

he could invent a way of weighing such a small thing. After a while thinking, he said, 'If you get a stick or something and balance it on something like this, then you can put the caterpillar on one end and weigh it against something on the other end.'

It was lunch time by now and he said he would think about it over his meal.

On returning in the afternoon he said that his father had explained that using Dean's method he could compare the weight of the caterpillar with something else, say a feather, but could not find its actual weight.

Talking over the problem, I suggested that we could weigh the creature against centimetre wooden cubes (part of some classroom maths apparatus) using a metre rule pivoted at the centre. We could then find out how much each cube weighed by measuring a number of them against a standard 50g weight. Dean liked the idea, so we followed this plan. Using the classroom scales 103 cubes balanced 50g. Jason, who had come to join us, said that this was near enough 100 and that then each cube must weigh $\frac{1}{2}$g.

We then pivoted the metre rule to balance at the 50cm mark. On one end we placed the furry caterpillar, on the other end the cube. The caterpillar weighed more than the $\frac{1}{2}$g cube. Using two cubes we saw that it weighed less than 1g. I suggested we cut a cube in half to make a $\frac{1}{4}$g weight. Using this we found it to weigh more than $\frac{1}{2}$g but less than $\frac{3}{4}$g. . . .

. . . (The following day) the caterpillar was again weighed as being between $\frac{1}{2}$g and $\frac{3}{4}$g. Dean suggested that we could halve the cube again to get a more accurate measurement. I agreed and added that we could even make further halvings. Thus, we soon had a cube, a half-cube, a quarter-cube and an eighth-cube weighing $\frac{1}{2}$g, $\frac{1}{4}$g, $\frac{1}{8}$g and $\frac{1}{16}$g respectively.

Dean has not yet come across fractions in his maths scheme. (Throughout the school children use workbooks from a graded primary mathematics scheme.) We worked together at the blackboard for a while talking about how to write and name fractions and the various relationships involved in the fractions we required. He had no trouble in understanding this.

Using the new weights and the ruler, Dean measured the caterpillar to weigh $\frac{1}{2}$g and $\frac{1}{16}$g.

We returned to the blackboard for more talk about how we might add fractions, using diagrams to help in the explanation. Leading him carefully through this and asking many leading questions, Dean soon found that $\frac{1}{2}$ and $\frac{1}{16}$ could be combined as $\frac{9}{16}$. Thus he recorded $\frac{9}{16}$g as being today's weight for the caterpillar. . . .

... I then suggested that since he had appeared to grasp ideas involved in fractions so well, he might like to find some work from his maths scheme on this topic. To my surprise, he took up this idea enthusiastically.

Dean is currently on Book 3 in this scheme (out of five graded books intended for use across the junior age range). He returned to me having found a Book 5 with a section on fractions. With practically no help from me he soon completed several of the tasks in this section. I do not wish to go into the details of this textbook work here, but merely to note that he had little difficulty in tackling an exercise that was 'theoretically' one or two years in advance of the book he is currently working on. I do not here imply that his current book is too easy for him. On the contrary, I have seen it to present him with considerable problems on several occasions. Nor do I wish to criticize this particular graded scheme, one which is in common use in many English primary schools at present. Rather, my point is that where a mathematical idea has arisen from a meaningful context, and one over which the child exerted an overall control of the objectives, he was able to work at an apparently higher level than might otherwise have been expected. Furthermore, the assumption that the various 'levels' of mathematical competence relate in a rigidly determined and hierarchical fashion is strongly brought into question if a child is able to 'skip' at least a full year in a carefully graded scheme and yet have no difficulty in tackling the tasks set, so long as such tasks bear a direct and understood relationship to the activity over which the child has been able to exercise control.

In this work, in the previous activity of his described and in many other instances of the children's mathematical investigations, I was struck by the rationality they brought to bear when coping with new tasks. Such evidence strongly contradicts the views of the connectionist psychologists according to whom, as Elliot Eisner remarks:

> One could not safely assume general transfer or the use of 'reason' as a way of coping with new tasks. As a result arithmetic text-books placed heavy stress on the catch phrase of connectionist psychology — 'practice makes perfect' — and 'recency', 'frequency' and 'intensity' became the guiding principles of effective pedagogy.[3]

Whereas the computations of Laraine showed her to have been working in a way which was largely irrational and accords with the connectionist viewpoint, Dean's strategy is both logical and orderly.

The difference in their approaches was not due to a difference in their inherent ability to be rational, but to the context in which they worked.

But the effect of my intervention in Dean's work should not be overlooked. Dean did not 'discover' the mathematical relationships involved in the fractions with which he worked. My instruction was deliberate and formal. His freedom to direct his own activity in the way which interested him most did not, in this case, lead directly to some 'natural unfolding' of his knowledge and skill. Rather, it provided him with a sense of awareness or consciousness of what it was that he needed to know about. Dean needed smaller weights to weigh his caterpillar; he needed to be able to name these fractional weights, write them and add them up, and he *knew* that this was what he needed. He was therefore prepared for the new knowledge and skills in which I was able to instruct him when he, implicitly, called for my assistance. It was this sense of awareness that resulted from his control of the activity and which was the missing element in Laraine's work.

Viewing Dean's learning as his response to a need for it accords with the findings of Luria in his experimental investigations of twins with speech difficulties. Concluding the account of his investigations, he writes: 'the results of our experiment show that, with the creation of an objective necessity for speech communication, the children were satisfactorily prepared for the acquisition of a language system.'[4] What I wish to emphasize here is the importance of the *child's* being aware of the objective necessity.

My argument here can be related to the idea of 'readiness' that is a common notion amongst teachers. It is usually supposed that a child is 'ready' to be instructed in a particular skill, for example, in the initial stages of reading, when certain other prior skills have been mastered. There is obviously some truth in this idea. But the crucial idea that these mathematical examples illustrate is that 'readiness' consists not so much in the children's mastery of a pre-specified set of skills, as in their awareness of the need for a new skill in order to solve their problems and an awareness of the form of this new skill. This awareness is perhaps most properly gained as a result of children exercising their inventiveness in situations which are significant for them. Once they realize, as Dean did when he came to weigh his caterpillars, that a certain new skill is required, then instruction can take place in such a way that the overall control of the activity is not taken away from the child. This argument suggests the close link between inventiveness on the one hand and the learning of conventions or techniques on the other. To suppose, as Bennett did, that a teacher emphasizes one at the expense of the other, is to fail to grasp this link. Similarly, to characterize teaching styles as being either 'didactic' or 'exploratory' (see p. 39) oversimplifies the complex role of the teacher who needs, by a constant process of interpreting the meaning of the children's activity, to be on the look out for those points in the children's growth where direct instruction is appropriate. The concept of the children's control that I have developed does not preclude the teacher's acting as instructor, but demands that instruction should serve needs of which the learner has come to a state of awareness. It is this awareness of need that is the point of growth.

Notes

1 BENNETT, N. (1976) *Teaching Styles and Pupil Progress*. See particularly the section of his questionnaire given to teachers which relates to their teaching of language.
2 See RUSSELL, B. (1946) *History of Western Philosophy*, p. 784.
3 EISNER, E. (1979) *The Educational Imagination. On the Design and Evaluation of School Programs*, p. 52.
4 LURIA A.R. and YUDOVICH, F.la (1971) *Speech and the Development of Mental Processes in the Child*, 107.

Chapter 7

Dramatic Quality in David's Writing: A Case Study

In the last chapter I focused on the point at which growth takes place, when the child realizes that a skill is needed and when invention has prepared the ground for the mastery of it. In this chapter I want to consider growth as a continuing process through a succession of such points. To do this, it is best to follow one particular line of development in one child's work as a kind of case study. This case study will also draw on the themes developed in the earlier chapters. The line of development it will follow concerns David's successive attempts, over a period of one term, to imbue his writing with a dramatic quality.

At the beginning of the year of my enquiry in Chris Harris's class, David was not a particularly enthusiastic writer. As the year progressed, however, he began to see writing as a more exciting activity. One important reason for this change in attitude was his realization that his writing style could take on a more dramatic quality by the use of direct speech. By exploring the different ways of using speech in prose writing he was able to make his stories more lively and new horizons concerning his purposes in writing began to open up.

In order to gain some insight into David's ability and concerns in writing at the beginning of the period in question, we might look at one of the most significant pieces that he wrote in the first term of the year. Through this piece one can see what it was for David to write a story. The conditions under which he wrote were 'ideal'. He wanted to write, he was able to work withdrawn from the distractions of the classroom and he was able to call on my assistance and involvement freely. Such favourable conditions were not possible to achieve in the later writings that will be discussed. There is little doubt that this first piece represents David's writing at its most successful prior to his work in the term under consideration.

Fieldnotes: 14 September

David has been spending much time over the last few days with this latest story. The work has been something of a struggle for him. It is unusual for him to spend so long on one story and he has exercised considerable self-control in resisting distractions and keeping at the work. I have been with him much of the time offering gentle encouragement and help with the spelling only when he asked for it.

The original idea for the story, and indeed the decision to write at all, was completely his own as is shown by the fact that he chose to write in his own personal exercise book rather than in his school writing book.

The story is not quite complete. David said that only a few lines were necessary to complete it.

A scientist called Dr. Snape lived in a hut in a forost. He had no friends. But one day he meet a boy his name was Paul his dad was an inventor one day Paul went to see his friend Dr. Snape. He was tring to invent a large bomb (1) Paul said doue you want some help inventing your bomb yes please said Dr. Snape so Paul went and got his Dad. Paul said to his Dad will you come and help my friend Dr. Snape yes said Pauls dad. So Paul showed his dad the way. Dr. Snape was in his laboratory working on his bomb when the door opened Pauls dad walket in. Paul shouted Dr. Snape! Dr. Snape got up to meet Pauls dad. Hello said Dr. Snape to Pauls dad and they set to work on Dr. Snapes bomb. Early the next morning Dr. Snapes bomb was ready. Dr. Snape rang up the prime minister I have a bomb that can blow up the would I will detonate the bomb if you dont give me what I want which is 60000000 pounds (2). The prime minister gos to see the roule family the queen says to prime minister give Dr. Snape the money. Dr. Snape rings up the prime minister again and tells him were to leave the money at the docks the prime minister agreas Dr. Snape gets ready to clecket (collect) the money the prime minister leves the money were Dr. Snape told him and gos (3) to get redy for an ambush. . . .

I recorded the following conversations at the points noted:
At (1)

R: 'What's Dr. Snape going to use his bomb for?'
D: 'He's going to use his bomb to get what he wants'
R: 'How?'
D: 'Going to threaten to blow up the world.'

R: 'But what does he want?'
D: 'Don't know. I haven't got to that bit yet.'

David has the general structure of the story in mind. The problem for him is how the plot is to develop in detail. The writing is obviously not going to be a personal piece which draws directly from his experience. Rather it is to be a piece of reporting of an imaginary event. Style is therefore directed towards concise description of the unfolding events rather than towards vivid imagery. Throughout the piece he was plagued not by the problem of 'How shall I put it?' but rather 'What happens next?' He always wrote quickly once he had decided what was to happen, but spent much time figuring out the plot step by step. At (2)

R: 'What's that large number you've written?'
D: 'Don't know. Its just a big number.'
   [I briefly explained how it came to be sixty million. This interested him.]
R: 'Is the prime minister going to give in to Dr. Snape's demand?'
D: 'Yes. He's gonna get in a panic — Can I put the queen in it?'
R: 'Yes, if you like.'
D: 'Yes, he's gonna talk it over with the queen and she gets worried.'

From this brief snatch of conversation one can imagine the scene. David readily uses phrases like 'talk it over', 'get in a panic', 'she gets worried', which bring the scene to life. But when it comes to the writing the vivid details are missed out. Why? Not because David had any difficulty in 'putting it down' but, I would suggest, because he thought such additions unnecessary. He was out for economy and accuracy in describing events which were, in themselves, exciting. 'Bringing them to life' was not his concern in writing about them. They were already alive in his imagination. I'm not here suggesting that he consciously decided not to use a more lively imaginative style but rather that, in this kind of story, such stylistic concerns were of no interest to him. Thus the event he spoke of is rendered blandly as: 'The prime minister gos to see the roule family the queen says to prime minister give Dr. Snape the money.'
At (3)
David spent a long time thinking here, becoming easily distracted but at the same time clearly wanting to get the next step in the plot right.

> *D:* 'I can't think how they're going to catch him.'
> *R:* 'Does he have to get caught?'
> *D:* 'You can't let the baddies get away with it.'

Perhaps this suggests that David is merely following a formula, that of the police catching up with the 'baddies' in the end. But as we have observed in much children's writing, it also expresses his moral concern. His imperative here is not only a literary one, but also a moral one (and also no doubt reflects David's view that in the real world the police always do catch the 'baddies' in the end).

The story seems broadly to fall into two parts. In the first part (the detail of Dr Snape's living in the forest and having no friends and the vivid description of Paul introducing his dad to Dr Snape), Paul and his father do add some colour to the narrative. But this is lost in the second part (once the threat is made). Paul and his father are no longer mentioned and the style becomes one of bland reporting. This change in style, which coincides with David's change from past to present tense, is somewhat uncontrolled but reflects a change in David's interest from the three initially main characters to the unfolding of the major plot. . . .

(Michael Armstrong, in a memo to these notes, suggests the reason for this: 'When the story moves out from the laboratory to the high political life it moves into an area of experience so remote from David that perhaps the style is *bound* to change. Within the laboratory, he could still conceive of the situation as parallel to his own family life. But it's the change from the intimate to the grandly public that he finds so hard to master. Not surprisingly.')

The following day David completed the story with a final sentence or two in which Dr Snape was ambushed by the police and sent to prison.

The story presents a fair picture of David's approach to story writing prior to the second term. For him, considerations of plot are paramount and often override any concern to view the language he uses with much self-consciousness or with a sense of audience. Details are considered of little importance, the 'life' of the imagined events remains largely in his mind, the story being an economical account of the events that are essential to the plot.

The first sign that David was beginning to grow out of this more limited approach to story writing occurred at the beginning of the second term. Towards the end of a day in the first week of term, David told me that he wanted to write but did not know what to write about. He recalled his Dr Snape story of the previous term, remarking that he would like to do another long story like that one. (Most of his writing in the intervening time had been relatively short stories or poems.) David obviously liked his Dr Snape story, so I suggested he start another adventure. . . .

Fieldnotes: 11 January
. . . David thought this a good idea. He then said, 'I'm not going to start it 'One day . . .' like I usually do. . . . But how then shall I start it?' I suggested that he could just omit the 'One day' and start with whatever would be the next words.

David thought for a minute in silence and then said, without any pauses: 'I know, this is how I'll start: "Sid said to his mum 'Can I go down to the brook with my friend Don?' Sid's mum said, 'Yes you can but mind you take your wellingtons and be careful not to fall in. And be back by six!'"'

(Note here the importance David attaches to the opening sentences. As in Dean's Farmyard story (p. 107) the opening has to set the context in which the narrated events take place.)

Straightaway David started writing:

> Sid said to his mum can I go down to the brook with my friend Don. Sid's mum said yes you can but be cear full wont you yes mum. Be back by 6.00!!! Yes said sid and his friend Don.

David then told me that he had left out the 'wellingtons' bit but that it did not really matter. He explained how the exclamation marks were very important by demonstrating how the mum would have made this command emphatically. I corrected his first upside down attempt at an exclamation mark.

He then said, 'Do you know what's going to happen next?'
I guessed, 'I bet he does fall in.'
David said, 'We'll see!' and continued writing:

> 'When they got to the brook they fownd it was very deep
> sid tripped on a old tin box sid said Don Don!!! come
> cwickly Don Look whot I fownd Don.

As David was writing this I was being 'led up the garden path' thinking that the reference to the deep water was going to affirm my expectation of Sid falling in. From the speed with which David wrote it was clear that he realized that this would not happen. He intended to mislead the reader, thereby heightening the drama. In fact, the phrase 'they found it was very deep' is irrelevant unless David does intend to lead the reader on, and David is the last person to include irrelevancies in his stories.

David told me how he had got the 'Tripping over the tin

box' idea from a TV story he had watched. In that story the child found a note inside the box saying 'meet me at the cliff-top tonight.' I asked him if there would be such a note inside this box. He said there would not. Instead, it would be 'rather like Alice in Wonderland', he said. 'When he opens the box everything will suddenly be quite different.' He continued:

> Sid got his pen knife out and opened the box sudley a big flash hapend and avrey thing changed they were in a big palace siting next to a king and queen and the king said whot are you dowing here well we dont now the king ordered the gardes to put them in the dungeons and be quick about it as well. When they got to the dungeons they found it was dark and damp. In the dungeon there was a big flash the two boys were gone.

By now it was time to go home. I asked David if he had any idea how it would finish. He said that there needed to be some kind of explanation, something to make the story make sense, but couldn't think of what. He would think about it at home and finish the writing the next morning.

When he returned to school this morning he finished the story without further discussion with me:

> They landed back near the brook. They went home and Sid's mum told sid off for being late home. That night Sid got sent to bed with no tea Sid's mum said that will tech [teach] him to be late home from the brook.

David was pleased, as was I, with this ending. The lack of explanation gives the story the 'Alice in Wonderland' character that he had intended. Mum's words of warning in the beginning and the final telling off give the story a perspective and a context. Note especially that the last sentence, 'that will teach *him* a lesson', is addressed to herself (or the reader,) as if an aside or epilogue to the story, and not to Sid as might have been expected. This increases its moralizing flavour and sets the narrative in relief. This is a child's fantasy, one which directly opposes mums and their commands and conditions. Yet David is not himself wholly a 'child' in that he can see the whole fantasy and its context in perspective.

Throughout the work David showed a kind of controlled self-confidence that I have rarely observed in his writing. He was confident not only with regard to the plot of the story itself (this is usually his chief concern) but also in his fluent use of language: 'Sid said, "Don, Don come quickly Don, look what I found Don"', the repeated 'Don' adding to the excitement; 'The king ordered the guards to put them in the dungeons, "and be quick about it as well"' is a sophisticated yet natural construction adding that touch of life which has so often been lacking in his earlier writing.

This piece represents a considerable development in David's story writing from the Dr Snape story of the previous term. It might be argued, however, that since in this later piece the plot was less complex, he was therefore able to devote more of his attention to other literary aspects and that it was this which resulted in his increased concern and success in these respects. But it should not be overlooked that David chose to write in this way. Although it was to be 'an adventure' as he said at the outset, he saw that the interest in writing such a piece consisted in more than merely the plot. In the way he leads the reader on to believe that Sid is going to fall into the brook, and the way he contrives the beginning and the ending, it is clear that David senses the audience. By 'audience' I do not mean any specific audience: to a large extent he is his own audience in this respect. But he is able to stand back sufficiently from the unfolding of the adventure in his mind to consider the perspective of the reader. It is this that allows him to reflect upon the smaller datails of speech and action and to express them in a way which, while appearing fluent and natural, is none the less deliberate and intentional.

David continued this interest in describing detail, and in particular the use of direct speech, in his next major piece of writing some two weeks later. He began to see how, through such detail, characterization can be developed.

The morning of the day in which he started this next piece had been spent visiting two museums in Leicester. One of these museums concerned clothing and in it there was, among other things, a shoe shop set in the style of the 1920s. In the little shop were· models of a sales assistant and lady buying a pair of shoes. David liked this display and soon began to improvize a conversation that might be taking place between the sales assistant and his customer. He put on an obsequious tone for the assistant and a somewhat snooty one for the lady. We then visited a replica of a draper's shop where David put on a similar performance.

Fieldnotes: 25 January
Later that day, when we were back in the classroom, David said he would like to write again. (David has been writing quite frequently this term and seems to be enjoying it much more than I recall last term.) When I asked him what he was going to write about he recalled the episode in the museum shoe shop and said he would write about that. I asked him how he intended to do this: was he going to write down the conversation which he had

imagined, or what? David replied that he could write it as an account of our trip. He said, 'When we went to the museum we . . .' and continued to tell me how the first few sentences might go. He then said he thought that to write it in this way would make for rather a boring piece. But then he didn't want to write the conversation on its own either. He said he would instead make it into a story. It would be about a man who gets a job at a shoe shop and the conversation would be between him and his first customer. 'I could start "One day . . .?"' said David, 'But I think I'll not start with "one day". Instead, I'll start it like my last story' (the adventure of Sid and Don.) David thought a little, then added, 'But how exactly shall I start it?' It seemed to me now that 'One day' had been excluded as a possible starter, he needed some other 'cue' for an entrance — something to get things started and to set the scene. I suggested he first thought up a name for the man, but did not add that he might start the story with that name. David quickly said, 'I'll call him Sim and start "Sim was looking for a job".' David then went on, without stopping for pauses, to recite how the first few sentences would go. His speech here was just as if he were reading something that he had written: fluent, but not sounding at all like an oral account, with short precise sentences. David then stopped his recitation and said, 'The only trouble is, if I carry on I will forget what I have said and so won't be able to write it properly.' So I suggested that, since he was clear in his mind what would happen, he should start the writing right away.

David got half way through the story before it was time to go home. He remarked on how he had written quite a lot but had not yet got to the important part, the conversation.

This morning David returned to school to finish his writing, but unfortunately I was not available to be with him. Later in the day he showed me the finished piece. He had received no help with spelling or punctuation and I shall record it here as he wrote it.

The Shoe Shop

Sim was looking for a job he was filling [feeling] a bit board — joust siting around all day Sim looked in the papers when he fownd a advertisement the advertisement said shoe shop assistant wanted come to 12 Jan Street. So Sim put on his cout and went to 12 Jan Street. Sim said can I see the manger [manager] please I am the manger said the man have you come for the job yes said Sim well the pay is 8 pounds I'll take it said Sim. So the next day Sim got up erely and went to work when he got

setled in he opened the shop his first cusmer [customer]
was a old lade. The old lade said I would like a pear of
swade shoes Sim said i have thees madam yes but have
you got them in a smaller size I am a frade not But we
have got a darker couler can I have a look yes said Sim so
he went away and cam Back with a Dark Brown pear of
shoes the old lade had a look at them and said have you
got them in lite Brown no said Sim But we have got some
lite gray no said the old lade I wont them in the lite
Brown But we have not got any lite brown shoes so the
old lade got up and went.

In many respects this is not a remarkable piece of writing.
Its simplicity verges on flatness. While David was quite pleased
with the piece, it was written in a somewhat hurried manner and
perhaps he has not explored the possibilities of the situation as
much as he might have.

But as far as David's development in writing is concerned
this piece is of considerable significance. It shows a continuation
of the progression, started in his 'Don and Sid' piece, away from
the concern for 'basic plot and no frills' towards a deeper interest
in the details of situations and personal relationships. This is the
first occasion on which I have known him to start writing when
he knew the complete plot of what he was about to write. His
aim in this piece is quite clear and he is completely conscious of
it: to write an account expressing a relationship between a shop
assistant and his customer. This is what had interested him in the
museum that morning, and now he was going to use writing to
explore and express that idea.

His choice of a context for the dialogue — that of an assistant
on his first day's work having previously been out of work — is
well chosen. It not only leads us to sympathize with the assistant,
but also adds to the anxiety which the situation puts him in. This
anxiety is further increased when Sim finds that the man to
whom he addresses his initial enquiry is himself the manager.
The sales talk of the assistant, which combines formal politeness
with a keen desire to sell the old lady something, is quite well
handled: '"I am afraid not, but we have got a darker grey."' The
scene ends with a certain feeling of exasperation on the part of
the assistant: '"But we have not got any light brown shoes." So
the old lady got up and went.'

These are only small points which, perhaps, David has not
exploited as much as he might have. But it is the fact that David
has considered such details that is significant; that he should
choose to write a piece which depends for its effect upon them.

David's deliberations about how he should write this piece are important. He saw that in order to satisfy his requirements for the form of the piece, he needed to transform his recollection of the episode in the museum in order to make it a story. Thus, one might say that the 'shaping' of his experience that the writing enabled resulted directly from his awareness of the different forms in which it could be represented. An account of the experience would not have been good enough. Only by putting it into a story can he explore its implications for characterization.

The sequence of events in David's writing and its development after this last story are considerably complicated by the fact that he had at least two pieces of writing on the go at the same time. However, I shall follow the writing in its chronological order, considering first the opening of his next piece which was concluded a week or so later after other pieces had been written.

David's interest in dialogue had been sparked off by 'The Shoe Shop'. In his next piece of writing he made it quite clear that he wanted to write another dialogue. He had become aware that in 'The Shoe Shop' the writing was somewhat difficult to follow because he had used no punctuation to signify the beginning and end of speech. It seemed that in this next piece he specifically wanted to practise the punctuation of speech. I briefly explained to him some of the conventions for punctuating speech. He said he was going to write about a stowaway who was discovered on board a ship 'in the olden days'. Once he had started the writing I offered him no further assistance and did not point out where his punctuation had gone wrong. This is as far as David got with this writing which was written ten days before this entry in the fieldnotes. The rest of the story is taken up at a later point.

Fieldnotes: 1 March

> "He's a stowaway"
> "No I'm not"
> "Yes you are"
> "Let's chuck him overboard"!!!
> "Let's whip him till he's rour"!!! "Whot's going on here"
> "We have found a stowaway"
> "Lock him up and I'll deal with him later but now get back to work." Later that day the captin went to the locked room an un locked the door
> "Get up"
> "No I wont"
> "I said get up"

From this opening to the story, it is already quite clear that

David had set himself a formal framework or objective within which to work. He is trying to minimize the narrative content of the story so that the story is as much speech as possible. David was quite conscious of this intention for he explained that while it is the captain who says, 'What's going on here?' it is not necessary to say so immediately in the narrative. If it is not already clear from the context, it is made obvious from the later lines, 'Later that day the captain. . . .' David also realized that a lot of 'saids' disrupt the flow of the piece and can be omitted.

This was the first time that David had asked me about punctuating speech. It is clear evidence in support of the earlier argument that the introduction of a new technique follows an awareness of the form in which that technique is to operate. For David had already grasped some very definite ideas about how he would like to use direct speech in his writing before he was concerned to learn the technical details of its punctuation. He then first explores the uses of this technique within his broader explorations of the use of dialogue in order to add to the dramatic content of his story writing.

But at this point David's interest in dialogue was not to the exclusion of all else in his writing. He still enjoyed fast moving plots in stories. He had written in dialogue form in order to bring situations to life, but had not yet given much thought to direct speech within a more complex plot. It was towards this that he turned in his next story. But, interestingly, his enthusiasm to write the story, and no doubt the more complex direct speech within it, led him to abandon the use of speech punctuation in this next piece. Nonetheless, the role that direct speech plays in it is most important.

Fieldnotes: 1 March
A few days ago David came to school saying he had a good idea for a story. It would be about a man who wants to marry a girl, but the girl is about to marry someone else. He learns of this a few days before the wedding, and during these few days hatches plans to entice her away from her proposed bridegroom. David did not tell me at the time, but during our conversations after he had written the story it transpired that his idea had come from a play he had watched on television the previous night. However, as David explained, his story differed from the television story in many respects although the basic theme was the same, as was the conclusion in which the bride is abducted by the hero during her wedding ceremony. No doubt David had omitted to tell me about the source of his idea because he thought that I would think it unoriginal to use the theme of a play he had recently watched.

Before he started writing David excitedly told me how the

man (Don, again — David said he like short names, they were easier to spell and quicker to write) would impress the girl. He would make her a super car. But in the end he would charge off with her on a white horse, just as she was about to be married.

He said he had a good idea for the start. This would not be 'one day' or anything like that, but would be the middle of an argument between Don and his beloved.

David wrote very quickly, finishing the piece in about half an hour. He asked for no help, saying that he was not bothered about spelling here. Also the 'inverted commas' were not going to concern him (as they had in 'The Stowaway'). He was concerned that nothing should interrupt the flow of his writing. The piece is titled in the index to his book of stories 'I want to marry you'.

I whot [want] to mary you well I don't whot to mary you!!! But I love you all the people stear [stare]. Well I'm getting marrid to Jim on Sunday. Don tourt [thought] to himself I've got 6 days to in press her or she will mary Jim. I now what Ill do Ill go and see her mother. Can you tell me whot Jill likes best well she likes cars so Don runs down the path and gets into his dads tow truck and when he gets home he has a idea. I'll desine a car for her so Don go's in to his dead [bed] room and start to draw this

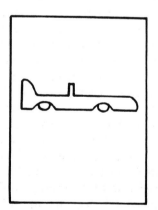

is what he Dhrow. It has a 3 leter engin and it can go 100 mph it has lerther seating and pine wood das.

So Don gets it made and tow's it down to her house and gave it to her. Whill she was looking at the car Don had a nother talk with her mother Whot does she think of marig well she thinks it is being picked up by a night in armer So Don went to get a night costume and hire a hours [horse].

Can I hire a hours here you shor can so Don hires a hours and rides in to check [church] just as the vicar says if any one knows just cause or impediment why this couple should not be joined together in holey matrimony he is to declare it now or foreever hold his peace. Jill I love you and they ride off.

The only part of the writing I did help David with was the

words the vicar says immediately before he marries a couple. I could not remember the exact words, but this sounded about right. David asked me if I could find out exactly what is said at this point. I shall take him a book of Common Prayer tomorrow. (David often expresses to me his atheistic conviction and opposition to marriage. Thus the plot is particularly comic for him.)

The super car which Don designs is a rough copy of one of David's recent drawings.

David has certainly succeeded in portraying the farcical nature of the comedy and his style here is fluent and racey.

The opening row is ingeniously constructed, being interrupted with the narrative 'all the people stare'. No longer does David need to introduce his characters by name, these easily emerge from the narrative. While he has not bothered to use speech marks, he has used direct speech very effectively. There are no unnecessary 'said Don's' in the story (a feature which seems to be so characteristic of children's writing where speech marks have been 'formally' taught). Also, the transition from direct speech to narrative is made easily.

David was also very pleased with the ending. Perhaps it seems rather a cliché to us, but no doubt not to David, and it is certainly very appropriate here.

The role of the speech in this story is crucial. It is not merely an addition to add 'colour' to the piece, but conveys the important facts and atmospheres in a way which is both economical and dynamic. The opening row presents the situation, with its feeling of added embarrassment, in a more accurate way than would have been possible without the use of direct speech. Then, by writing directly what Don was thinking, we are told enough about the plot with economy and without disrupting the flow. Perhaps David over-used the direct speech when Don hires the horse: '"Can I hire a horse here?" "You sure can."' This appears to add little to the story and could well have been either left out or else elaborated upon in order to fill out the plot. But if this is a valid criticism it should not surprise us. For now David no longer conceives of a story as being the narration of a sequence of events, but the representation of a drama being enacted in the mind of the writer and the reader in which the thoughts and speech of the characters play the major role in the life and meaning of the events. With this change in emphasis, or conception, it is to be expected that the balance between direct speech and narrative is not yet quite achieved.

After finishing this piece David immediately returned to his earlier story, 'The Stowaway'. This he completed over the next two days. For clarity, the whole of this story is transcribed here using the original spelling and punctuation.

Fieldnotes: 6 March
1. "He's a stowaway"
   "No I'm not"
   "Yes you are"
   "Let's chuck him overboard"!!!
5. "Let's whip him till he's rour"!!! "What's going on here"
   "We have found a stowaway"
   "Lock him up and I'll deal with him later but now get back to work." Later that day the captin went to the locked room and un locked the door
10. "Get up"
   "No I wont"
   "I said get up"
   "Why? do you whot me to get up"
   "Because I want you to scrub the decks then you can furl the
15. sails" So Jack got up and set to work. First Jack got a bucket of soupy water and started to scrub the decks after he had doun that he climbed the mast and startid to pul the big hevey sail up then he went to see the captain. "Whot shall I do now sir" you can go and get some supper then you can
20. light the lamps and then get in to your hammock and get off to sleep"
   "Yes sir
   So Jack goes of to get some super and starts to light the lamps
25. "Do you want some help Jack"
   "Yes please"
   So John gets a lighter and starts Just as John was going to light the last one.
   "Oi! whot are you doing helping Jack"
30. "Because I could not get of to sleep captain"
   "Jack why did you let John help you."
   "Because I was tired"
   "You will both be whipted tomorrow morning." the next morning John and Jack got woke up by two very heftey
35. looking men John got tied to one of the masts and Jack got tied to the other mast. the tow men with whips started whiping the two men tied to the masts. When the punishment was over the two men toke them back to ther hammocks to sleep. When they woke up.
40. "Agh! my back hurts does yours Jack"
   "Yeah it does harf sting"

in comes the captain
"Jack you help unfurl the sails and then you can have some
brekfust John you help pull up the anker and then you can
45. have some brekfust"
When they reached land
"Oi! Jack lets xckepe [escape] while we can"
So they go of and ther is no one that has seen Jack and John
ever again.

David's awareness of what he was doing was made very clear
by several of his remarks. Quite unprompted by me, he said at
one point while writing that his story consisted of 'bits of
speaking' and 'bits of not-speaking'. The 'not-speaking' bits
explained what could not be explained by the 'speaking' bits. He
then told me that 'said so- and -so' could often be left out.
Indeed, in his manuscript, the words 'said Jack' have been
crossed out by David after 'Yes please' (line 26). He went on to
explain other points at which it was unnecessary to refer directly
to the speaker. Particularly sophisticated devices are used to
avoid direct reference in lines 40–41; 43–44; and 46–47.

The narrative in David's writing here plays the part similar
to that of the action in a performed play. And this is indeed how
David saw the whole of this writing. The story is viewed in terms
of the speech. (David was very concerned, in lines 40 and 41 that
"Agh!" and "Yeah" should be spelt as they would sound.) It is
thus appropriate that 'said' should be omitted and David has
succeeded in organizing the speech so that this does not result in
any ambiguity in the reading. This avoidance of ambiguity would
not have been possible if David had written the story exactly as a
play would be written (only avoiding the name of the speaker and
the stage directions). Thus, while it has the dramatic effect of a
performed play, a transformation is made so that it suits the
requirements of a written story. I don't mean here that David
intended to write a play transformed into prose form, but rather
that in writing a piece of prose he realized that a racey and
dramatic effect could be achieved by writing as if a play were
being enacted before his mind's eye. This convention, though a
discovery for David, leads him to being confronted by various
problems (for example, of ambiguity and continuity) which he
successfully and deliberately tackles. (One might consider the
comic strip as being another form which tackles the same
problems in a different way.)

The development in David's skill of adding dramatic quality to
his writing by the use of direct speech, and its relationship to his
awareness of the literary forms he uses, is most apparent in these

pieces. But it would be misleading not to view this development in the light of their subject matters. While in 'The Stowaway' David does have a formal objective in mind and is also concerned to practise the conventions of punctuating speech, this piece is not merely a formal literary exercise. The subject of which he writes is appropriately treated in the form that interests David. It describes a triangular relationship between the authority figure (the captain), the anti-authority hero (Jack) and the hero's accomplice (John). Such a theme throws up the moral problems of punishment, helping the underdog, obedience, etc., problems with which David has considerable concern in his day-to-day living. Such a theme and such problems are naturally explored and expressed within a dramatic context: they are indeed dramatic aspects of life. This same appropriateness between the subject and its treatment can be seen in the comic-farce of 'I Want to Marry You' and the situation comedy of 'The Shoe Shop'.

There is a two-way relationship here between the growth of David's skill and the subjects of his stories. While he selects themes which are appropriate to the use of direct speech in writing, his interest in this skill is in response to his enthusiasm for representing and thus gaining an understanding of such dramatic aspects of life itself. This development of skill, together with an understanding of its appropriate application, is made possible by his growing awareness of the literary forms in which it may operate. Such awareness is achieved by a process of deliberate exploration and innovation in his writing, a process which both requires and demonstrates David's control over the growth of his own skill.

Chapter 8

Epilogue: Sharing Our Understanding

Reflecting upon his work, some three years after writing *Closely Observed Children*, Michael Armstrong wrote: 'I believe that educational theory finds its most appropriate expression within the practice of sustained description.'[1] The emphasis I have placed upon my descriptive accounts of some of the activity of the children in Chris Harris's class reflects the same belief that it is by describing rather than by naked theorizing that we gain some insight into the child's mind. Nevertheless, it is through these descriptions that threads of theory emerge. The attempt to tease out these threads is an essential part of the reflective process which is at the heart of an enquiry. Just as Ian had to take a step back from his experience of measuring in order to reach a more enlightened view about the mid-point of his aeroplane wing (p. 72), or Helen and Karen 'operated upon' their experience of the bridge when they came to write about it (p. 100), so we also must, at times, take a more distanced view of our descriptions of classroom life. But Michael Armstrong's comments suggest a warning: that any attempt to set too great a distance between the descriptions of the particular and the theory which underlies or emerges from them will inevitably lead to theorization which is sterile, leaves the child and the classroom out of focus and can play little part in our practice of teaching children and understanding them.

It is with this warning in mind that I want, in this chapter, to try to draw out some of the threads of the argument about learning that have emerged in the previous chapters. I use the word 'learning' here, rather than 'children's learning', quite deliberately. For as the enquiry has progressed, it has become increasingly clear to me that, granted the limitations of experience and knowledge in the young child, there appear to be certain principles which underlie the learning of adult and child alike, and certain concerns that each express as they strive to make sense of their world through investigation, representation and communication. As we closely observe and reflect upon the attempts of a child to understand a new experience, or to cast her imaginings into written form, we readily draw parallels with our own experience. I suspect that these parallels can be drawn more closely than is commonly recognized, and that we can more usefully extrapolate from our understanding of the children's learning to our understanding of our own learning, and vice versa.

This focus on our own learning as teachers will lead to the second theme I want to explore in this chapter. Traditionally, research is seen as being followed by a process of dissemination. By following the development of the Leicestershire Insights into Learning project, which was set up in conjunction with this enquiry, I shall suggest a different approach to the sharing of understandings from that presupposed by the traditional research/dissemination model; one that is perhaps more appropriate to the teacher's classroom enquiry and which relates more directly to the professional development of teachers in schools.

In the first chapter I drew a somewhat simplified distinction between transmission and interpretative approaches to teaching. From an interpretative approach, which underlies the analyses and argument of the ensuing chapters, a central theme to emerge is that of the children's control over their learning. The children's control over their activity consists in their awareness as to its purpose (or developing purposes) and their acknowledgement of themselves as being a judge as to its value. It is most clearly manifested in their play and play-like activities. Inasmuch as useful learning results from children's play, this learning follows naturally from the demands of the activity itself. Children's play thus presents us with a paradigm of learning which the teacher, by interacting with the child, can seek to exploit. This confirms the view of Piaget, who, conceiving of education as a process of adaptation recommended that teachers 'seek to encourage this adaptation by making use of the impulses inherent in childhood itself, allied with the spontaneous activity that is inseparable from mental development.'[2]

The idea of 'conversation' is suggestive of the way we can encourage this natural tendency to learn without taking control away from the learner. By fostering a 'conversational' relationship with children we can enable them to reflect upon their activity, by presenting them with new ideas, alternative perspectives on their work and by setting up a dialogue. But, as 'conversation', such interaction recognizes that children will reinterpret our suggestions, intentions and ideas. This process of reinterpretation highlights the unpredictable nature of learning (and also of conversation), making it impossible for us to narrowly determine what learning will result from a sequence of interaction. However, its recognition is vital since it is by this means that children transform our ideas into a form which is appropriate to their experience, thereby enabling them to make sense of our ideas and use them in such a way as to confirm their control over their activity.

From this emphasis upon the learner's control I do not mean to suggest that, as teachers, we should not play a direct role in stimulating the children, in confronting them with new knowledge and in directly instructing them. Often, in the course of pursuing their own objectives, children will reach points where they need instruction from the teacher, or indeed from another child, in order to meet those objectives. In such cases, we may view the immediate control over the activity as being temporarily delegated by the child to the teacher (or to another child) for the period of instruction. We are, as it were, a resource which the child can either explicitly, or by means of implicit cues, call upon, when the need arises. Where new activity is initiated by the teacher, control over it must be handed back to the children at some point, by encouraging them to make their own reinterpretations of its purposes in order that the ideas can be related to their existing knowledge and concerns.

This idea that learning is controlled by the learner presupposes that knowledge is not transmitted directly from teacher to learner, but that it is reconstructed by the learner. It demands that both teacher and learner recognize that the subject matter of learning resides outside their 'circle of intimacy', rather than exclusively in the teacher.

In respect of the material environment of the classroom, control over their work is established by an active process of selection and interpretation of materials in terms of their present states of experience, interest and knowledge. Control would be denied were their activity to be merely a passive response to externally applied stimuli. Within the course of extended activities, children make successive interpretations and reinterpretations of their work. In this way the activity develops, with vague notions becoming clarified, unclear aims becoming focused and a general increase in the order or structure of the work. This developing structure may of course be threatened by the limitations imposed by the materials themselves, or by unforseen circumstances. However, often such intrusions provide a state of disequilibrium which itself challenges children to re-evaluate their work, view it from a new perspective and thereby gain new insights and awareness.

When the children were confronted with a wide range of experiences, such as on a field trip, we saw how this attempt to create order led them to construct hypotheses, or systems and 'pictures' in order to explain initially disparate phenomena. At this age, this approach tends to integrate a wide range of disciplines combining scientific and imaginative aspects.

Such relationships with the material environment may be seen as the attempts of children to gain an intellectual control over it and also a practical control over their work.

So far, I have traced this theme of the learner's control in relation to the external human and material resources of the classroom. But we can also see learning as being the attempt to control the internal life of thought and imagination. In respect of this inward life, control consists in a sense of awareness. What our evidence suggested was that even at the age of 9 or 10, given the external conditions of control, children are able to demonstrate an awareness not only of the subject matter they investigate, but of the very form of their investigation. A level of abstract thinking was apparent in which they were able to stand back from the immediacy of their experience (be it a scientific enquiry, a practical task or a 'philosophical' debate). They appeared able to operate not only upon the materials with which they worked, but also upon these operations themselves. Such thinking foreshadows what Piaget described as formal operations. It appeared to be important, for this level of thinking to be expressed, that the children make their *own* abstractions within a language context which is theirs. These are important elements of the children's control over their investigations.

I interpreted much of the children's scientific activity as closely paralleling that of the adult scientist, with hypotheses being framed, tested, refined and even, at times, deductive reasoning being employed. It appears that the young children's work, as scientists or philosophers, was limited not so much by any limits in their cognitive style as by the limitations of their knowledge and experience. The plausibility of viewing the children's activity as like that of the adult scientist depends upon our recognition that the children may be working at the frontiers of their understanding.

Writing is another process through which control is exercised, for by representing the world in written language the writer reflects upon it with a higher level of awareness. When children write about their experience, or their imaginings, they are not merely recording them. They make that experience or image objective to them — they stand back from its immediacy — so that it may be shaped or transformed by being written. In this respect, the children's writing contained this same element of operating upon their experience as did much of their practical and scientific investigations.

Children like to write about the unusual, whether imagined or real. What was striking in this kind of writing was that the process of writing appeared to be largely directed towards relating the unusual to more everyday experience. Children, like adults, enjoy fantasy, but fantasy, to be meaningful and significant, must have its roots in reality. Story writing seeks to provide this relationship, and so, through their imaginative writing, children are brought to newer understandings of reality. This was particularly evident in those stories in which the children were led, through the process of writing, to consider characterization and the 'eternal' problems of the human condition. This approach to the interpretation of children's writing, which seems justified in that it allowed sense to be made of their stories, leads one to view the child writer as confronting the same kinds of literary issues as confront the adult writer. It is also a process through which children operate upon, and gain a degree of control over, their imaginative powers, powers which are, arguably, at the heart of the intellect.

Through my attempts to interpret the children's classroom activity I have now sketched out two aspects of their control: first, its outward manifestation as an attempt to control their own learning activity in relation to the external material and human world; and second, its inward manifestation as an attempt and process by which they gain a degree of control over their intellectual and imaginative powers.

In my understanding of how growth takes place, these two aspects of control are brought together. Outwardly, skill is seen as arising and being developed in response to the requirements of the activity and its goals. Rather than being an aspect of development which requires practice in isolation before it can be used towards creative ends, it in fact emerges in response to those ends. Its development takes place within a context which provides not only motivation for its practice, but one which enables the child to see its purpose and develop an awareness of it.

This awareness of a skill, or rather, the awareness of a need for a skill, appears to be an essential condition for its emergence. An awareness that there is something we need to know, a skill we need to master or a convention we need to adopt is a starting point for further growth. It is the inward aspect of the need for control. Following the children's work, it appeared that this awareness grew as a result of their inventiveness. As the children invented ways of resolving their problems, so they became prepared — or reached a 'state of readiness' — for new knowledge. Thus inventiveness and the mastery of conventions are not opposing aspects of learning, but on the contrary, the one paves the way for the other. To suggest that a teacher emphasizes the development of skill rather than the development of creativity, or vice versa, is to fail to recognize this close relationship between them. Children cannot invent all that they need to know. But invention can bring them to an awareness of the form that newly required knowledge might take. It is as if it shapes a space in the child's understanding which is thus made ready to accommodate new learning.

A role for the teacher at these points of growth should be

apparent. We have to watch out for cues from the children that this state of awareness has been reached. Through 'conversation' we attempt to promote it and to elicit cues. Such cues may be interpreted as an implicit request by the child for control to be temporarily delegated to the teacher (or indeed to another child, book or other instructional resource) for a sequence of instruction. It is important that this control be handed back to the child at an early stage, so that any new knowledge gained can be reinterpreted in terms of the child's activity and its purposes, her broader experience, and can be incorporated into her expanding repertoire of inventiveness. Only then will instruction confirm the validity of invention as being the source and motive for learning, rather than undermine the inventiveness which children are so eager to bring to the classroom in the early years of their schooling.

I have now drawn out the central strands of argument that emerged from interpretations of some of the children's work in Chris Harris's classroom. Many of these ideas had begun to take shape in my earlier classroom practice and were suggested by the accounts which Michael Armstrong gave of children's work, in my own classroom, in his book, *Closely Observed Children*. They thus represent not the product of a research project in isolation, but the present point in a continuing struggle to understand children by teaching them, which is given focus and direction by means of a sustained classroom enquiry.

I now want to turn to the question of how these ideas have been shared and developed with other teachers. But first, I must make some general remarks about what I mean by 'sharing ideas', or 'dissemination' as it is called in the research world. When ideas are shared, learning takes place. Therefore, in attempting to share our ideas about children's learning, one might expect that any of the ideas about the nature of learning in general (for example, the feature of control) which emerged from work in the classroom, would be mirrored in the learning situation which developed between the teachers. One particular aspect of teaching and learning that underlies the present enquiry is the idea that interactions between teachers and learners should, in principle, be critical. That is, that each party should engender a questioning approach, contributing criticism from their own experience, with the expectation that the ideas of each party are open to reinterpretation and change.

It follows from the above that any proper sharing of our enquiry with other classroom teachers would necessarily bring with it the opportunity for the reinterpretation, modification or refutation of the ideas embodied in that enquiry. For each teacher would have their own experience of teaching and learning which would have no less a claim to validity than ours. Furthermore, if these teachers were to come from a wider range of school backgrounds, the experience they would bring would further extend the scope of the enquiry.

It was with these expectations in mind that, while I was still working in Chris Harris's class, we decided to form a Research Consultative Group (RCG). This group consisted of fifteen teachers drawn from a wide range of Leicestershire schools, from a special school for primary-aged children with learning difficulties, to an inner-city comprehensive of predominantly black students. The teachers in this group would, we hoped, consider the material which Michael Armstrong and I had gathered, critically reflect upon the interpretations we were making, and contribute from their own classroom experience. They had been contacted informally, having expressed an interest in the enquiry, and met about twice a term with the support of the local education authority.

A pattern soon began to emerge to these early meetings of the RCG in 1978/79. Michael Armstrong or I would present some children's work for consideration — a story, a painting or an account of the investigations of a small group of children — together with our interpretations of it. Usually these presentations would meet with considerable support from the other teachers. As two teachers who had had the opportunity to analyze in more depth than is possible for those in normal circumstances, our interpretations of the meaning and significance of the children's work were often thought to be plausible and interesting. As the main issues of our enquiry were shared through these presentations, there appeared, in general, to be a good deal of agreement about the directions in which we were going.

However, underlying this general agreement and apparent corroboration of much of our analysis, I began to feel that these discussions were insufficiently critical to provide a useful check on our work. It became increasingly clear that underlying our descriptions, and indeed any descriptions of classroom life, lay a framework of understandings which was hidden and could not be easily exposed. We presented selections and interpretations, rather than 'raw data' from the classroom. Our writings, like those of anthropologists, were 'themselves interpretations, and second and third order ones to boot.... They were thus fictions; fictions, in the sense that they [were] 'something made' .... not that they [were] false'.[3] The problem for the Research Consultative Group was not that they wanted or expected totally objective or uninterpreted and unselected samples from the classroom. The general approach to classroom enquiry as described in Chapter 1 was not in dispute here. No, the problem was that, accepting that our writings were necessarily 'fictions' in the above sense, they needed to know more about how they were 'made' in order to assess, critically, their significance.

This difficulty which the RCG faced has parallels with the difficulty which Dean, the child in Chris Harris's class who investigated the taxonomy of caterpillars (see p. 26), overcame through the process of investigation. He needed to find out what lay behind the business of grouping his caterpillars in order to discover the principle of taxonomic classification. Only when he had done this, in his own way, did he make use of the reference book (p. 57) in a way which he could control, now that he could understand, in principle, how its information might have been gathered. It had been Dean's reluctance to accept my original strategies for sorting his caterpillars, and his determination to follow his own path, which led us both to consider some of the logical complexities that underlie classification. In a similar manner, only by developing their own strategies for describing and interpreting children's work (within the broad outline of classroom enquiry), could the teachers in the RCG begin to confront questions concerning the frameworks of understanding that are necessarily involved in the process of making descriptive accounts. Only then could they provide a critical perspective on the accounts that Michael Armstrong and I had been presenting.

Realizing this, the group decided to become more heavily committed to collecting, describing and interpreting material from their own classrooms. Obviously, it was not possible for full-time teachers working on their own in their classrooms to conduct enquiries on the scale that Michael Armstrong and I had done, but even the occasional attempt to select, closely describe and analyze some sample of children's work enabled the participants in the group to appreciate and debate the perspectives that play such a determining role in this kind of enquiry. Based upon their own experience of this, they were then more able to reinterpret the interpretations of classroom life that were presented to them. Furthermore, by collecting material from their own classrooms, the range of schools from which children's work could be examined was broadened, thus extending the applicability of our emerging ideas to a more general sample of classrooms and teachers.

It also became clear to many of us that the value of what we were doing was not only determined by the 'results' of our enquiries — our developing understanding of children's classroom activity — but by the process of enquiry itself. As I argued in Chapter 1, the process of enquiry can be an integral part of our teaching, though a part which is, perhaps, severely constrained by the pressures of time and space under which we practise. However, deliberately focusing on this enquiry element for some of the time, and sharing it with other teachers, would appear to have a direct effect on how we understand our own teaching. Thus, by extending the group of teachers who contributed (albeit in a small way) descriptions and reflections upon work from their classrooms, we were not only strengthening the 'research' base of the project, but were, in effect, embarking on an in-service education programme.

Appreciating the in-service potential of our classroom enquiries, Leicestershire Education Department in 1980 agreed to support an extension of our work. I was appointed to coordinate the Leicestershire Classroom Research In-service Education Scheme, a title which was later changed to the Insights into Learning project as it became increasingly apparent that the term 'research' had misleading connotations for many teachers and was an inappropriate way of describing much of the work which later began to develop in schools.

The general aim of the project was to provide a variety of opportunities for teachers to investigate, more intensively than would normally be possible, some aspect of the children's learning in their classrooms, and to share their investigations. Since 1980, the project has extended in three directions. First, the RCG has developed as a forum for the analysis of material from the classroom. Second, the education authority agreed to provide for at least two additional teachers each year to conduct classroom enquiries, along the lines that Michael Armstrong and I had done, on secondment in colleagues' classrooms. Third, steps have been taken to stimulate groups of teachers within individual schools to conduct classroom enquiries as part of their school-based in-service programme. Following the progress of these three aspects of the work may suggest some of the possibilities, and some of the problems, that are confronted when groups of teachers attempt to exert a controlling influence over their own learning about classroom life.

Over this period the membership of the Research Consultative Group grew. As the members became more involved in collecting and sharing their interpretations of material from their own classrooms, so the work became less focused on the enquiries that Michael Armstrong and I had conducted. Also, as the material gathered became more diverse, so the enquiry came to mean different things to different teachers. For some it provided an opportunity to evaluate innovations that they were trying out in their classrooms; others were more concerned to develop appropriate methods for gathering and analyzing material concerning children's understanding; yet others wanted to articulate the implications for good classroom practice. In accordance with the principle that we as teachers should, like our children, exert a degree of control over the purposes and methods of our own studies, it was important to allow for this diversity of aims. We therefore split the RCG into several sub-groups, each of about six teachers, which defined their own themes for investigation. While these sub-groups work autonomously, part of the RCG's meetings is devoted to the sub-groups sharing their work with each other by making presentations of papers and classroom material.

Each of these sub-groups is made up of teachers from both primary and secondary schools and from different disciplines. This has led to an interchange of ideas which is not normally possible. It has enabled us to see that many aspects of learning and understanding are not specific to any particular age or curriculum area. For example, a story by a 7-year-old at the beginning of her writing career and that of a talented 15-year-old writer can equally be analyzed in terms of their attempts, through writing, to order their experience, to relate it to the wider issues of life, and to grapple with the problems of literary form within the constraints of their literary technique, thereby extending that technique. Such an approach to children's writing has enabled us to give meaning to material from a wide range of schools. It would seem to provide significant support to the assumption, which underlies my analyses of children's writing (see Chapter 5) and Michael Armstrong's accounts in *Closely Observed Children*, that children's work should be interpreted as a serious intellectual and expressive endeavour. Furthermore, this sharing of our interpretations of children's work from a wide range of areas has begun to dispel many of the myths concerning the difference between primary and secondary-aged children, or between the arts and the sciences — myths determined more by the institutions of schooling and society than by the human need which they supposedly serve.

While the enquiries of the RCG have been necessarily limited by the pressures of time on the classroom teacher, the work of those seconded for a year to conduct fieldwork alongside colleagues have developed more or less freed from normal classroom pressures. These teachers on secondment have emerged from the Research Consultative Group and continue their membership of that group while on secondment and afterwards. This ensures that they start their fieldwork with some sense of direction and with a degree of shared experience with the other teachers and feed back their experience to the group. Their enquiries have ranged widely from an investigation of the multi-cultural influences in the artwork of children in a predominantly non-white inner-city primary classroom to the development of scientific understanding amongst a group of 15-year-olds. However, the wide range of subject matter is linked with a common approach which emphasizes qualitative descriptive accounts from the perspective of teacher-as-researcher and attempts to get behind the overt behaviour of the children to the understanding and concerns which underlie it. They usually work with a colleague who is also a member of the RCG and therefore shares an interest in the enquiry. Leicester University has supported proposals for the seconded teachers' studies to be reported in the form of research MEd. theses.

The seconded teachers meet once a week together with those who were seconded the previous year but have since returned to the classroom. These meetings have several functions. They enable experience to be passed on from one year to the next, thus furthering a sense of continuity and development to the enquiries. They act as a mutual support group to those confronting the difficulties of developing rigour and focus to their analyses, and also to those who have returned from the reflective and critical atmosphere of full-time investigation to the pressures of the normal school situation. They also act as a kind of committee at which decisions can be made about the future work of the project as a whole. However, the central purpose of these groups is to develop our understanding of children's work and how we should analyze it. At times we will sit around a child's painting trying to pick out the significant features in it. At others we grapple with such notions as 'consciousness' and 'intention' (as, for example, in the question: 'Was the child consciously intending to paint this feature in this way?'). Such discussion soon becomes philosophy. But it is a philosophy which is rooted in the children's work, whose application to the classroom is immediate and therefore whose ideas can be appropriated by us. These meetings are often characterized by considerable difference of view, sharp criticism, and even deliberate polarization in our positions. But such dispute, far from threatening the well-being of the group, serves to confirm its identity in the struggle to make sense of the children we teach and the social context in which we teach them. It represents an attempt to create for ourselves the kind of learning environment which we would aim to build with the children, one in which we equally teach and learn from each other and collaborate in our control of that process. The knowledge which results from this process makes no claim to ultimate objectivity, nor is it the private property of the individual. Rather it aims at an intersubjectivity founded in shared experience and shared commitment.

The meetings of the RCG and of the seconded teachers take place outside the school setting. The participants are individuals, from a wide range of schools, who share an interest in this kind of enquiry. Without the pressures on time and space, and freed from the hierarchical relationships that characterize the society of the school, it has been possible to construct an open environment for self-education. But the ultimate aim of classroom enquiry must be to enrich, rejuvenate and even radically to reconstruct the curriculum of the children in school. There are narrow limits to what individual teachers, however enlightened by their own classroom enquiries and experiences with a wider group of teachers, can do to influence the school as a whole, unless their work is shared within the school. As the earlier attempts of Michael Armstrong and myself to share our enquiries with other teachers demonstrated, this does not mean simply telling colleagues on the staff what they have done, or presenting them with accounts of the children's learning they have observed. It requires that other members of staff also become involved, even if only to a small extent, in the process of classroom enquiry itself, thus institutionalizing classroom enquiry within the school.

The extent of the problem of sharing insights gained during extended classroom enquiry with other staff has been suggested by the reports of seconded teachers who have returned to their normal teaching role. Typically, they appear to feel a sense of frustration, isolation and perhaps alienation, even though the school has given sympathetic support to their secondment. Their appetite and faculty for critical reflection about children's learning has been sharpened, but on return to the school, with its constant pressures, it receives little opportunity for expression with other teachers. Staff have to meet regularly in order to discuss timetabling, examinations, parent evenings, and all the other managerial issues that demand immediate decisions. The discussion of children's learning through sharing classroom enquiry rarely produces immediate and tangible results. Therefore, even though the desire to understand children may be a prime motive of teachers, it tends to be the 'soft centre' of educational practice, the part which yields most to the increasing pressures of school life.

The work of the Insights into Learning project points to further reasons for tackling this problem by institutionalizing classroom enquiry within shcools. Although it would be facile to view the activities of the teacher and those of the children as though they were separable aspects of classroom life, the kind of enquiry reported here has, as its prime focus, the activity and understanding of children, rather than the performance of the teacher. We have found that directing our attention in this way allows for a less threatening situation when we come to share our analyses with colleagues. For it is not directly our performance which is open to challenge, but our understanding of children. Nevertheless, any attempt to interpret children's work leads us to make more explicit and articulate the educational values which inform that interpretation. In this way, a group of teachers can explore those values upon which their teaching strategy is based, without necessarily feeling under pressure to defend the way they perform. Within the context of a school staff, this means that the values and aims upon which the curriculum is constructed can be made explicit and opened for critical review. All enquiring teachers would contribute to this review from the basis of their close observations of children. Such a development would raise the classroom anecdote to the level of the rigorous case study, thereby transforming it into a powerful tool for curriculum change.

It is with this aim that plans are now being made for groups of teachers to set up enquiries within schools. The experience of these school-based groups would then be shared with the RCG which, together with the seconded teachers, will continue to develop strategies and frameworks for observing and understanding children. In this way it will be possible to complete a continuing cycle of development which extends from the classroom, passes through the more rigorous discipline of sustained enquiry and returns to influence the school.

But an 'open' in-service education programme demands the same kind of struggle as the 'open' classroom. As the distinctions between researcher, teacher and learner become blurred, so a higher investment is demanded from all participants. The functions of production and consumption in educational research, traditionally separated by the institutions of research and schooling, become finely interwoven within a new social context. One aspect of this demand is that we, as teachers, must learn to write about our experience of the classroom, our interpretations of the children's work, our educational values, with the confidence that we have something significant to say and that our experience is valid. For most of us our own schooling has not prepared us for this. Many of us in the project have experienced a profound resistance to writing which cannot be explained merely by lack of time, motivation or 'technical' ability. It has more to do with the fact that the majority of our writing experience in academic institutions has been for the purpose of being judged by others rather than as part of a genuine sharing of ideas. We have to learn that we each have something to write about classroom life. As we begin to do that, so we shall be building for ourselves and our students the most powerful tools for improving the quality of that life.

Is not our problem here like that of the children at school whom we expect to write from their own experience? To give them a better start than we have had, we must appreciate and respond to their writing as an act of communication, rather than as a product to be measured and graded.

Like many of the themes within the project, we find the children's difficulties reflected in our own. The struggle of learning is in principle the same.

Notes

1 ROWLAND, S. (Ed.) (1983) *Teachers Studying Children's Thinking*, Number 2: A collection of articles on the analysis of children's work in the classroom, p. 41.
2 PIAGET, J. (1969) *Science of Education and the Psychology of the Child*, p. 151.
3 GEERTZ, C. (1975) *The Interpretation of Cultures: Selected Essays*, p. 15.

Bibliography

ARMSTRONG, M., *Closely Observed Children*; London, Writers & Readers, 1980.

BENNETT, N., *Teaching Styles and Pupil Progress*; London, Open Books, 1976.

BRUNER, J.S., *Toward a Theory of Instruction*; Mass., Harvard University Press, 1966.

DEPT. of EDUCATION and SCIENCE, *Primary Education in England*; London, HMSO, 1978.

DEWEY, J., *Art As Experience*; New York, Capricorn Book, 1934.

DONALDSON, M., *Children's Minds*; London, Fontana Collins, 1978.

EISNER, E., *The Educational Imagination: On the Design and Evaluation of School Programmes*; London, Collier Macmillan, 1979.

ELKONIN, D.B. and ZAPOROZHETS, A.V. (Eds), *The Psychology of the Pre-School Child*; Mass., MIT Press, 1971.

FLANDERS, N., *Analyzing Teacher Behavior*; Reading, Mass., Addison-Wesley, 1970.

FLAVELL, J.H. *The Developmental Psychology of Jean Piaget*; Princetown, New Jersey, Van Nostrand, 1963.

GALTON, M., SIMON, B., and CROLL, P., *Inside The Primary Classroom*; London, Routledge & Kegan Paul, 1980.

GARDNER, D.E.M., and ISAACS, S., *The First Biography*; London, Methuen, 1969.

GEERTZ, C., *The Interpretation of Cultures: Selected Essays*; London, Hutchinson, 1975.

GLASER, B.G. and STRAUSS, A.L., *The Discovery of Grounded Theory: Strategies for Qualitative Research*; Chicago, Aldine Publishing Co., 1967.

HAWKINS, D., *The Informed Vision: Essays on Learning and Human Nature*; New York, Agathon Press, 1974.

JACKSON, P.W., *Life In Classrooms*; New York, Holt, Rinehart & Winston, 1968.

JONES, A. and MULFORD, J. (Eds), *Children Using Language*; London, Oxford University Press, 1971.

LURIA, A.R. and YUDOVICH, F. *Speech and the Development of Mental Processes in the Child*, London, Penguin Books, 1969.

NASH, R., *Classrooms Observed*; London, Routledge & Kegan Paul, 1973.

PIAGET, J., *Science of Education and the Psychology of the Child*, (translated by Coltman, D.) London, Longman, 1969.

PIAGET J., *Six Pschological Studies*; London, University of London Press, 1964.

POPPER, K., *Objective Knowledge: An Evolutionary Approach*; Oxford, Clarendon Press, 1972.

ROWLAND, S., *Enquiry Into Classroom Learning*, (Unpublished MEd thesis) Leicester University, 1980.

ROWLAND, S., *Teachers Studying Children's Thinking, Number 2*; Leicester, Leicestershire Education Department, 1983.

RUSSELL, B., *History of Western Philosophy*; London, George Allen & Unwin, 1946.

VYGOTSKY, L.S., *Thought and Action*; Mass., MIT Press, 1962.